ADVENTURE CARAVANNING WITH DOGS

DOGS 'N' DRACULA

JACQUELINE MARY LAMBERT

Copyright & Disclaimer

Contact:

Facebook:@JacquelineLambertAuthor

Amazon:www.amazon.com/author/jacquelinelambert

A Road Trip Through Romania

Adventure Caravanning With Dogs

Dogs 'N' Dracula

Jacqueline Lambert

I would like to dedicate this book to the kind and generous people of Romania.
We visited your wonderful country in its centenary year.
Thank you for your warm welcome and for your part in making memories that we will cherish forever.

BY THE SAME AUTHOR

Adventure Caravanning with Dogs Series
Year I – Fur Babies in France – *From Wage Slaves to Living the Dream*
Dog on the Rhine – *From Rat Race to Road Trip*
Dogs 'n' Dracula – *A Road Trip Through Romania*

Forthcoming Title
Pups on Piste

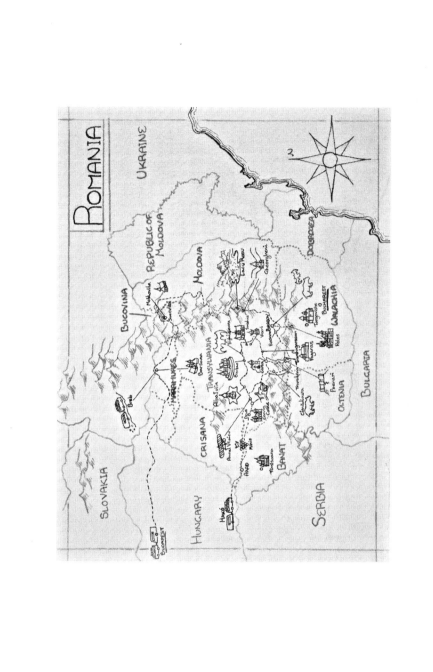

PROLOGUE

"You'll be kidnapped by gypsies and eaten by bears."

"Packs of wild dogs will attack – if the wolves don't get you first."

"You'll be robbed, scammed, and you'll have to bribe officials."

"Terrible roads, awful drivers – and this year, there have been floods and riots."

And what about those vampires?

As a dog- and caravan-friendly destination, Romania was not the first place to spring to mind.

It was three years since Mark and I gave up work to hit the road with Big Blue, our trusty Hyundai iLoad van and 'Caravan Kismet' ('Fate'), a Bailey Unicorn Vigo. With Big Blue brimming with windsurfing equipment, we were heading for Spain and Portugal, but decided to turn left, lured by magical landscapes and more than twenty-five World Heritage Sites. I can't deny that it was with trepidation that we crossed into

Romania with our four Cavapoos (Cavalier/Poodle cross) – Kai, Rosie, Ruby and Lani. Well, there was always Plan B – turn around and go elsewhere.

However, from Day One, we experienced nothing but kindness. We went for the 'full' Romanian experience: magnificent medieval citadels, fortified churches and Dracula's birthplace; we discovered Romania's El Dorado; crossed the Carpathian Mountains via the Transfăgărășan – 'The Best Road in the World' and adopted a Transylvanian orphan...

We named him Blade, The Vampire Slayer.

The Fab Four became The Famous Five when we were told that the affectionate, little, black stray probably wouldn't survive the winter. So, before his first birthday, Blade received toys, his first lead, collar and tag, a microchip – and a passport to a new life in England.

Thirty years after the fall of communism, we felt privileged to see a country in a time of transition; modernising rapidly but still in touch with its history, tradition and the past.

And, haunted by a satnav with a revenge complex, it is fair to say that as Adventure Caravanners, we truly did achieve our objective: 'To Boldly Go Where No Van Has Gone Before.'

MEET THE GANG

Mark and I met through an adventure club. At the end of our first date, the conversation went thus.

"Can I see you again?"

"I might consider it!"

"It's up to you. I won't ask again."

I had met my match! Hastily, I said yes.

Thirty-seven days later, I said yes again when Mark popped the question. Meeting Mark was like re-connecting with an old friend and to be honest, if he hadn't got a move on, I was going to propose to him.

You might notice a hint of impulsiveness about us, although when you know something's right, why hesitate? It's the same as falling in love with a puppy, or spotting the caravan-of-your-dreams lurking at the back of a dealership on a day out...

Mark and I waited a respectable thirty-seven weeks before we got married. We lamented that our respective employers would not grant us leave for full-time adoration, although latterly, we addressed our career-related separation by working together. From the moment we met, we felt blessed to share so many likes and aspirations; adrenaline, the outdoors, the same kind of movies and music, we both prefer wild places over touristy hell holes and hate shopping, unless it involves buying sports gear.

We learned to windsurf together and ski to a similar standard. What separates us in sport is not ability, just a slightly different approach to risk. My beloved is 6' 6" tall, powerfully built and believes that he is invincible, while my sense of our mortality is an uneasy bedfellow with my overwhelming tendency to overreact.

Despite the passage of time, seeing how we interacted happily and tenderly prompted a stranger at the gym to collar me in the changing rooms to ask,

"Is that a new man in your life?"

She reeled in disbelief when I told her that we had been married for eighteen years.

Some say that marriage is not a word, but a sentence. That Mark and I get on so well is fortunate, particularly now that 24/7/365, we are confined in a metal cell on wheels.

We were both made redundant in our early fifties and, after buying that caravan-from-the-back-of-the-dealers and celebrating with two bottles of champagne, we decided to give up work, rent out the house, sell most of our possessions and tour in her full-time. We did this partly because retiring to travel was a long-held dream. It is very difficult for me to admit in public to the second part of the reason, but here goes. We were both suffering from severe, clinical depression.

For more than a quarter of a century, our working lives had consisted of stressful, high-pressure jobs with challenging targets. It had taken its toll. Once the corporate world had chewed us up and spat us out, we were really quite poorly. We had to find a way to support ourselves without a salary, because we were both too ill to have considered any form of alternative employment.

If we learned anything from our professions, it is that there are no problems, only opportunities. Ten-hour days and a 200-mile round trip commute (I know – I can't believe it either!) were not conducive to sharing our lives with a dog, so as soon as we gave up work, we put that right.

Extensive breed research revealed that Cavapoos would suit our lifestyle. A cross between a Cavalier King Charles Spaniel and a Poodle, the Cavapoo was everything that we wanted; lively, affectionate, intelligent and small enough to travel easily. Poodle crosses are very popular as they tend not to moult, although they can be needy and suffer separation anxiety. This was no problem. As early retirees, we were perfectly placed to grant full-time adoration to puppies, as well as each other.

The intention was always to get two dogs. Kai, our black-and-white boy from Lincoln joined us a week before Rosie, a white-and-black girl from Chorley, near my home town of Blackburn in Lancashire. Kai means 'the ocean' in Hawai'ian, an element close to any wind-surfer's heart. Kai Boy loves three things; his bed, his ball and most of all, his Dad. Kai and Mark share an exceptional, once-in-a-lifetime bond.

Rosie is named after the AC/DC song *Whole Lotta Rosie*. She is a larger than her brother, since she is crossed with a Miniature rather than a Toy Poodle. Rosie is a fun dog, filled with the sort of exuberance that you wish you could bottle. Laid back and easy going, she takes everything in her stride. Rosie can teach you all that you need to know about life.

With a pair of pooches to keep each other company, our fur family was complete. Except that Mark fell in love with another woman.

"Three dogs is madness!" I proclaimed when he suggested that the little red puppy that he had seen when we picked up Rosie should join us.

I held out for two full days until I rationalised that if you have one dog you have a commitment. Two? Three? What's the difference? And the red puppy was very gorgeous. So, for the second time in a week, Mark drove from Bournemouth to Chorley and beautiful princess Ruby came into our lives. Although Mark chose her, she is very much a Mummy's girl. She loves paddling and frequently forgets that she is a princess. She returns from most walks slick with mud.

But we are 'that couple with four dogs', so what happened next?

Mark continued looking at puppies on the internet.

So, when Lani, a tiny, black bundle of mischief and fluff from Bury St Edmunds joined us three months later, I put up no resistance. Her name means 'heaven' or 'the sky' in Hawai'ian. Although she is the smallest and the youngest, this feisty little poppet keeps the whole pack in line. While Kai, Rosie and Ruby love a cuddle, Lani demands affection with menaces. 'The Paw' comes into play the second that you falter with the tummy tickle.

That was three years ago and now, we can't imagine life without The Fab Four. The unconditional love and joy that they bring worked instant miracles on our state of mind. Although Mark and I used to mock those who treat their animals like kids, we are now among the worst offenders.

We are often asked, "How do you manage with four dogs?"

The answer is discipline. Cavapoos made this easy – all of them walked off-lead from day one and Lani never needed formal training. She picked up every command simply by copying her siblings.

Regarding the humans, however, the discipline was woeful. 'No dogs on the sofa' and 'No dogs on the bed' were out of the window within days.

It goes against all doggie training advice and I am sure that some of you will recoil in horror, but drifting into slumber with Lani's furry face against mine, or Rosie's dainty Northern snores gives me a warm, gooey feeling. Lazy lie-ins with a coffee and a fur baby snuggle makes the morning a favourite part of our day.

Sometimes, Ruby starts up a little howl and everyone joins in, while Kai greets every new dawn with a look of shock, like a newborn opening his eyes on the world for the first time and trying to comprehend what on earth could have happened.

As Charles Schultz of *Peanuts* fame put it: "Happiness is a warm puppy."

Well, that's got the introductions over. Now, let's hit the road!

Lani, Kai, Rosie and Ruby at Corvin Castle, Transylvania.

BEACON 6 & BRITTANY – POOLE TO PENTHIÈVRE, FRANCE

The Curious Connection Between Chocolate & Polar Exploration

6am and our ferry, *Barfleur*, slid across a Poole Harbour so smooth that it seemed almost solid. The water glistened and flashed, reflecting the sunshine like a diaphanous, sequinned gown being pulled slowly across a mirror.

Poole Harbour is very shallow, so large vessels have to be guided through the shipping lane. A small boat accompanied us across the harbour.

"Do you think that's our Pilot boat?" I asked Mark.

"I doubt it" he replied. "It's got 'Captain Cod' written on the side."

Barfleur glided past Sandbanks, home to some of the most expensive real estate in the world. Even so, we decided that whoever had parked a helicopter in their garden was a bit showy-offy.

Our precious puppies were home alone in the caravan for the crossing. Although it was early morning, I was relieved that they were on the west (cool) side of the ship. Never one to overreact, the recent heatwave had left me worrying for days that they would all die of heat exhaustion during the crossing.

As the view of Poole Harbour diminished behind us in the wake of the ferry, we felt the cares and stresses of the last few months at home gently slipping out of our consciousness. The tingle of excitement of a new adventure was building. Once again, we were destined for freedom. We were Living the Dream.

...

Neither of us really knew Spain or Portugal. Mark had visited Majorca as a child in the 1970s, when Can Picafort and Magaluf had hardly a hotel between them and long before the terms 'binge drinking' and 'Shagaluf' entered the urban dictionary. More recently, he had played golf in Portugal, but had not seen any of the sights. Despite travelling extensively on six of the seven continents, I had yet to set foot in mainland Spain or Portugal. My logic had always been to keep Europe up my sleeve for when I was too old and decrepit to backpack around the world. Now, the onset of the many paws precluded any long-haul travel, so the plan was to head south over land and 'do' Iberia properly.

As on our two previous trips, our first stop was at Camping Municipal Penthièvre, near Carnac in Brittany. A wonderful campsite, right on the beach over-looking the magnificent sweep of Quiberon Bay, it is the perfect spot to meet up with the Seavets, a sprightly group of veteran windsurfers who never fail to give us a run for our money on the water.

We set up Kismet, our home for the next few months, next to one of these veterans; a charming, softly spoken English gentleman. Russell was a former Royal Marines Commando, who had also been involved in a number of famous chocolate commer-cials in the 1970s, performing some incredible stunts to deliver the mysteries of the box that 'the lady loves'.

"I broke my leg water-skiing in one ad, but I didn't notice until the next day!" An impressive list of injuries came to light as we got to know him. Russell was a master of understatement and stiff upper lip. "I once spent a whole week setting up a collapsing bridge, then the Director asked for a slightly different camera angle. I told him it was 'not easy, but do-able.' I spent two days adjusting the set-up, but it didn't work. As soon as I started the test, I knew that it was wrong. All I remember is the cameraman laughing his head off as I slammed into the mountainside. He said that I just swung towards the rock wall saying; 'Oh dear. Oh dear. Oh dear.'"

Russell invited us over one evening. He cycled to the supermarket for the ingredients, then cooked us a delicious Thai prawn curry. After dinner, he showed us a short documentary about Robert Cundy's 1962 Cape Britannia Expedition to Beacon 6, a cairn at the mouth of the Back River in the Northwest Territories of Canada. The purpose of Cundy's 900-mile expedition was to discover whether anything had been left at the cairn by Sir John Franklin's lost Arctic expedition of 1845. The documentary followed Cundy and three other men travelling through the Arctic, equipped with lightweight kayaks and woolly jumpers. One of those men was Russell.

"The rapids were huge; some too dangerous to run. We had to portage around these, carrying the kayaks, then making several return trips to carry the rest of our equipment. It was really rough terrain. At one point, we had to build a functioning kayak from the wrecks of two others that had been smashed by the rapids."

After weeks of gruelling hardship, Cundy's expedition found Beacon 6. There, they did discover a note. Left by the Canadian Geological Survey, who had been there two years previously, it confirmed that no Franklin relics had been found.

Oh dear. Oh dear. Oh dear.

But such is the life of a traveller. So often, things don't go according to plan. As we were about to find out.

A CHANGE OF HEART – AND A CHANGE OF DIRECTION

We were heading south to Spain & Portugal – but decided to turn left

The hottest things in the universe are gold particles smashing together in the Large Hadron Collider.

But that is only 7.2-trillion degrees Fahrenheit. Even if you added lovely, lovely Professor Brian Cox (or my beloved), which would definitely make it hotter, it wouldn't get close to the temperatures attained by the inside of a caravan pitched in full sun.

Mark had ridiculed the tiny, plastic, 12v fan that I had purchased from Amazon for £14.99, but as the temperature in Brittany sweltered away in the mid-30°s, it was a godsend.

Caravan Kismet's windows open upwards and outwards, hinged at the top, but there was hardly a breath of wind. I swathed the Perspex with towels and sarongs to keep out the blazing rays. Thus shaded, we could keep the windows open without the temperatures reaching the trillions-of-degrees, but it was still uncomfortably steamy for most of the day. At night, the fan made sleep possible.

Then we met a Dutch guy who lived in Portugal, our proposed destination.

"Temperatures there are breaking records. It's 50°C! There are forest fires. People are dying."

Mark and I reviewed our plans to head south.

"I saw Steve earlier. He has spent loads of time caravanning in Spain. He said that we would definitely need air conditioning there in July and August."

"We could head east; what about northern Italy? Or Romania and Bulgaria?"

"The forecast says that they're hotter than Brittany!"

I am an English Rose from the north of England, with a complexion that afforded me the nickname 'Mrs Milk-Bottle'.

"If it doesn't cool down *a lot*, it will be purgatory. It's too hot to do anything here. I only went outside for half-an-hour and I got sunburnt. I haven't been sunburnt for years!"

Besides the heat, we had no internet. Our MiFi internet hotspot had stopped working. In quick succession, Three sent us about twenty emails, saying that we had exceeded our roaming limit and that we owed a fiver; ten quid; eight pounds fifty; two pounds... before it finally settled on forty pounds, more than double the cost of our monthly subscription. The thing had barely worked since we arrived less than a week ago, so we rang Three to explain. They waived the charge, perhaps a little too readily.

This phone call to dispute roaming charges became a monthly ritual. Regardless of usage, we were charged extra every month, even when Three applied a cap to our data usage. During that phone call, they explained that, even though they were a technology company, they couldn't guarantee that the cap would work.

Thank you, Three. How about a company re-brand to 'Chocolate Teapot'?

Our bikes, windsurfers and SUPs (Stand Up Paddle Boards) stood idle in the still, oppressive heat. I felt guilty lazing around, reading, writing and doing very little, although I did enjoy it. Mark assuaged my guilt.

"This is our life. Not a holiday. We must do as we wish."

In our third year of retirement, I couldn't believe that I still harboured a work ethic.

The forecast promised windsurfing, so we stayed on in Penthièvre for a couple of extra days, but the flaccid windsock atop a neighbour's campervan said it all.

And so, because of the blistering summer temperatures down south, when we did set off, we turned east to follow the road less travelled. Well – less travelled by Brits than the one heading to Spain, at least.

PENTHIÈVRE TO POITIERS; CAMPING DU BOIS, CHALANDRAY

The Motorhome & The Footpath plus The Greenwich Meridian

With no particular goal in mind, we headed in the general direction of Chamonix and the Mont Blanc Tunnel. Rather than racing through the countryside on the toll roads, we opted to travel via the 'A' roads. It was an incandescent, sunny day and the scent of haymaking, cut grass and honeysuckle drifted in through Big Blue's open windows.

Our driving enthusiasm waned at Chalandray, near Poitiers, so we pulled into Camping du Bois de Saint Hilaire. There were two campsites nearby, but we thought that Ferme de la Naturiste might be best avoided if we wanted to preserve our modesty.

The campsite at Chalandray was owned by an English couple, Henry & Katherine. Running a campsite in France was how they were Living the Dream.

They were not the only outpost of Blighty in this part of France. The Greenwich Meridian, 0° Longitude, ran through the woodland surrounding the site – a pleasant, shady leg-stretch for the doggies. I stopped for a chat with an English couple, Patsy & Rod and discovered that they had responded to my recent caravan forum post about our proposed trip next year to Russia, Poland and The Baltics (assuming we didn't turn south and go to Spain.) They had loved Poland, and suggested that we contact Mir Corporation, a tour company who specialise in visas, bookings and itineraries for some of the more 'challenging' countries to the east of Europe. We shared stories, and they told me about a satnav mishap in which their motorhome had been guided over a mountain on a footpath:

"Of course, once we started, we couldn't reverse or turn around, so we *had* to continue. We were so close to the mountain on one side that we lost our fuel cap. We have double wheels at the back, so on the other side – the one with the sheer drop – only the inner wheel was on the path. Luckily, the front wheels were a little more inboard – and thank *goodness* that the edge of the path didn't give way. It did eventually open out on to a road. When the campsite asked which way we had come, the receptionist was horrified. She said, 'You can't take cars down there!' We told her that we hadn't. We had taken a motorhome!"

...

Caravan touring gives unprecedented access to nature. Kismet is a real home from home. She is equipped with a tall fridge, a four-ring hob and a microwave. To accommodate Mark, who is 6' 6" tall, along with four small dogs, we modified her bed to super king size. (Dog owners among you will recognise that despite this, we spend our nights clinging desperately to the edge of the bed, while the dogs stretch and luxuriate on memory foam and Hungarian goose down.)

However, the main reason that we chose Kismet was her wonderful, full-length picture windows at the front. Through these, we have been soothed by the Adriatic lapping the shore, just feet away and have watched mighty rivers, such as the Thames, the Loire and the Rhine meander by. Sometimes, our door will open on a pine forest, or mountains so high that their craggy peaks loom through the rooflights.

It was so relaxing to lie on the bed, contemplating our green cocoon of forest. I could see nothing but trees through the skylights and windows. The wind whispered in the branches, to accompany the sound of birds and cicadas, while the sweet smell of fresh grass drifted in with the breeze. In the caravan, we were also removed from people – their demands and expectations. I had read a blog about someone who had chosen the life of a hermit. After the Fidose of Reality that greeted the homecoming from our previous trip – which included a boundary dispute, a robbery, an assault, several fines, a home wrecked by tenants and substantial damage inflicted on Kismet by an oxyacetylene torch during an attempted theft from storage – I could understand why.

PARADISE FOUND! CAMPING LA CHASSAGNE, AUVERGNE, FRANCE

In the Laid-Back Land of Lentils & Volcanoes

I tend to fill the kettle and leave it on the hob the night before. In the compact living space of the caravan, this means that I can just lean out of bed to switch it on for my morning coffee.

The occupants of the tent next door were up early. It was 7:30am. A whiff of toast wafted into the caravan. I love the morning smells of a campsite. In Britain, the delicious sizzle of bacon frying...

My reverie was interrupted by the shrill screech of the smoke alarm. I shot out of bed. The kettle was still cold. Half asleep, in semi-darkness and without my glasses, I had turned on the grill rather than the hob. Crumbs in the grill pan explained the smell of toast as they heated up to the point of incipient combustion. Thank goodness for the smoke alarm. Otherwise, *we* might have been toast.

It was not a relaxing start to the day and the morning progressed along similar lines. Big Blue had come to life in a puff of blue smoke that morning and was getting through a lot of oil. We filled up with fuel at a Super-U supermarket, but they didn't sell oil.

The towing gear had also started making strange grinding and creaking noises. We pulled into a layby to investigate in a systematic manner: address tangle of bungee cords and cable locks on the bike rack at the back of the van; bikes off; me driving forward slowly while Mark listened; stop; shake the hitch; drive forward slowly; nod head; rub chin; repeat; conclude that you have absolutely no idea what the problem is; put the bikes back on; re-apply tangle of bungee cords and cable locks; marvel at the discovery of yet another new and unique bungee permutation; continue on your journey, thinking that the tow hitch will explode and result in untold carnage (me) – or will be completely fine (Mark).

With stops to buy baguettes, something for dinner, finding another garage to fill up Big Blue's oil and water, it took us a while to make any headway towards our destination.

Destination. Ah, well now, here's the thing. We didn't have one.

You might think that we didn't have a plan. Well you're wrong! We always have a plan. Without a plan, we'd have no idea what we were deviating from. This time, we changed our minds a few times then decided on the Auvergne.

The Auvergne is very, very pretty. We took a chance by stopping at Camping La Trouvé, a site with only seven pitches. Run by a Dutch couple, it was gorgeous – but unsurprisingly full. The owner, Monique, kindly recommended another, larger campsite, which she said might have lots of children. She must have seen my face drop, so she rang a Dutch friend nearby, who ran a natural site similar to Trouvé; Campsite La Chassagne, in a tiny village called Ronnet.

Marie-Anne welcomed me from an archetypal French farm complex which exuded age. Flowers tumbled around the grey, antiquated stones and chickens were pecking at the cobbles.

"How many nights?"

"Not sure."

"How many dogs?"

"Four."

"Let's call it two…"

I liked this place already.

Marie-Ann introduced me to her dog, Inchie, a friendly, soft-coated black-and-white chap with lop ears.

"We thought he was going to be small. That's why we called him Inchie. He had tiny paws when he was a puppy."

She walked me through the important features of the campsite – we went to meet the chickens and the sheep. They were small, rather like the rare and ancient Scottish Soay sheep, although they were a French breed. I fed them handfuls of grass while chickens hopped on and off their chocolate-coloured rumps.

The site had large, shady, secluded pitches. Ours overlooked a field of Charolais cows and calves. Every morning, a little red chicken wandered around the site, looking for treats. The 12th-century tower in the village stood proud in the trees above the campsite.

There was a delightful, Hansel-and-Gretel walk in the woods straight from the site.

"I've seen the location where I want my treehouse – overlooking a little river." Mark shared his dream.

It was so peaceful and, being under Dutch ownership, extremely relaxed. We were not looking over our shoulders waiting to be ticked off the moment one of our dogs moved a whisker. In fact, we were encouraged to let them off their leads; a wonderful and highly unusual freedom.

This really was Paradise Found.

I discovered the showers and toilets. Marie-Anne hadn't mentioned any of that during our tour – I guess she presumed I was capable of finding them. I preferred that she had showed me the sheep.

...

The area was teeming with attractions. We visited the Roman Bridge at Pont de Menat and walked up to Chateau Rocher. We took the SUPs on the River Sioule and ran a few rapids. As ever, the Pups on SUPs in their brightly-coloured buoyancy aids attracted plenty of attention.

After a halcyon week, rain was forecast so we decided to move on. I was disappointed that we hadn't got around to seeing the volcanoes in the Puy de Dôme, home of Appellation Contrôlée Puy lentils. Still, it was a good excuse to come back.

July 14th loomed. France's most important Bank Holiday, Bastille Day is not a good day to be on the road. We'd let that storm pass, then make our break for the border. Our aim was to cross Italy before the hideous, holiday mayhem of August was upon us.

5

CAMPING DE L'ÎLE CHAMBOD TO GRAN PARADISO, ITALY

On Boldly Going & The Quirks of Campsite Facilities

My day kicked off with four ten-second bursts of freezing cold water, full in the face.

The shower cubicle was so small that it was impossible to avoid the icy jet; so small that I had been unable to close the door once I hung my wash bag on the hook inside.

Campsite showers are a law unto themselves. While we have a lovely shower in the caravan, its tank supplies only eight litres of hot water, all of which we have to collect and empty ourselves. It's a bit of a faff, although that is not the main reason that the shower stands idle between bouts of cleansing fox-poo-smeared dogs.

The Law of Sod dictates that, whatever precautions you take, the water is *guaranteed* to run out the second that you are fully lathered in soap. Inexplicably, at this point, your partner is always unavailable to refill the Aquaroll water container. As such, we generally tolerate the many quirks and peculiarities of on-site facilities.

Sometimes, you can be lucky and get a luxurious wet room, with a proper shower mixer and a never-ending supply of hot water. Sometimes you get a pathetic trickle from a scaled and rusting shower head that you have to hold in your hand.

Some showers can inflict GBH. On the Continent, the hot and cold are frequently reversed. Try to adjust the temperature and the result is either cold water shock or third-degree burns. One campsite shower nearly gave me a black eye when the heavy metal chain that released the water came adrift and socked me around the head. Then, there's the scourge of timed lights or motion sensors. These inevitably plunge you into blackness the moment you are naked, wet and fully foamed.

At Chambod, the ten-second blasts were self-inflicted by the repeated pressing of a button. The water cannon was cunningly built into the wall at head height, facing the cubicle door. Ten seconds of water is rather miserly in a shower, but it did mean that each freezing face-full was mercifully short.

Campers have many elaborate solutions to short-burst showers, involving cable-ties and all kinds of paraphernalia. My top tip is to keep one buttock pressed against the button to maintain a continuous flow of water – taking care not to brand yourself on the scalding hot pipes.

We had left Ronnet for Camping de l'Île Chambod on the River Ain. The Ain was gorgeous: deep turquoise and green. Had we been able to get anywhere near it, we might have stayed more than one night.

Every part of the river frontage was private. I trespassed accidentally when I took the dogs into what looked like a park. Benches sat invitingly under trees, right on the river bank. A cooling, canine swim was just the ticket in 33°C, but when I turned around, I panicked. We had wandered into a private club and were imprisoned behind a heavy-duty security gate. I acted nonchalantly, rapidly weighing up my options. When I spotted someone sliding the gate to one side to let out a car, I made my move. The pack and I made a bolt and slyly slipstreamed our way out.

There was a bridge over to the Île Chambod, through a turnstile with a charge of €3 per person. I can't tell you if the island itself yielded any river access, since dogs were not allowed.

So once again, we moved on. We got up-and-at-'em and were all packed and ready to go by, oooh, 11am... Then Mark asked:

"Where is the pass for the Mont Blanc Tunnel?"

I have a high degree of entropy. Although I derive peace and satisfaction from rigid organisation, I am blighted by my natural tendency towards untidiness bordering on chaos. Mark has overcome this over the years. Not through any sort of husbandly nagging or arm-twisting, simply by tidying up. If I fail to put away my bits and pieces according to a rigorous system of 'a place for everything', I will probably never see them again. Unless I search in unlikely locations such as the fridge – or in a couple of still contentious cases – the charity shop.

"That looks like my pasta maker in the window!"

Silence.

"That IS my pasta maker!"

"You never used it!"

"How could I? I never knew where it was *because you'd put it away!*"

Mark's random approach to tidiness has led to a multitude of Magic Markie Moments involving the loss of keys, passports and other articles of critical impor-tance. Therefore, I do attempt to retain control of such items. Unfortunately, the system had failed with the tunnel pass, which had been put away in a 'safe place'.

"It's a good job I'm not an angry man!" Mark observed as, for the second time that day, he repacked Big Blue with all our worldly goods. I thought it prudent to avoid naming the mastermind behind the location of the 'safe' place.

...

The drive was exquisite enough to be added to the list of places to which we will have to return. It rose through the Bugey Valley, with her limestone escarpments and vineyards. We wound through quintessential French villages before briefly catching a glimpse of the flyover that usually speeds us through to the Alps on the Autoroute Blanche. To make headway, we did use some toll roads, but nipped off at Bellegard to avoid a traffic jam.

The satnav is great; it is a special, caravan one, which takes into account our dimensions. However, it can't predict roadworks. The centre of Bellegard looked like it had been hit by a meteor. The diversion routed us around tight turns that were nothing short of miraculous with a caravan in tow. We followed narrow streets with high kerbs and barriers; we even negotiated a car park and a housing estate before getting back on track.

The burnt-coke smell of Big Blue's straining clutch accompanied the climbs through the stunning hills of the Haut Jura National Park. After passing meadows bright with flowers, we slipped into Switzerland and dropped into Geneva, where a congestion miscalculation became evident. Although I was cheered by my first view of CERN, home of the Large Hadron Collider (and occasionally, Professor Brian Cox), we soon hit a monstrous traffic jam in the city. In general, I would say that there isn't a day that can't be improved by the sight of a particle accelerator – or the thought of Brian Cox – but my joy was short-lived. As we hopped back on to the autoroute, I noticed too late the sign on the slip road: 'Vignette Obligatoire'.

"We need to buy a vignette to use the autoroute..."

An electronic vignette or sticker must be purchased before driving on certain roads in some European countries. I was horrified, not that there was much that we could do about it. We were already in free fall down the rabbit hole and heading inexorably towards another fine. The only difference was that this time, our transgression had taken place in Switzerland, one of the most notoriously efficient and expensive countries in Europe.

Sick with anticipation that at any moment we would be relieved of the GDP of a Banana Republic for using three miles of Swiss motorway, we fled back towards the sanctuary of France. I thought that our number was up when we hit the Swiss Customs station, populated by heavily armed and uniformed guards. However, they simply smiled and waved us through the border. We crossed back on to French soil with a full wallet and a sense of deliverance. With our history of budgetary Armageddon, our bank account groaned with relief.

The Mont Blanc tunnel spilled us out in Italy, where we chose the scenic route. Despite passing this way often, we usually missed the beauty of the Aosta Valley, hurtling through on the main road via a system of tunnels. The plan was to camp near Aosta itself, but a slight error of scale meant that our campsite was an hour's drive up a side valley, in the Gran Paradiso National Park.

The drive was jaw-dropping, both in terms of scenery and the scary-hairy-pins. At times, I could look down and see the previous bit of road directly beneath me. We snaked up, then down to Introd, before ascending Val Savarenche on a set of intestines, which emerged at Campsite Gran Paradiso: 5,971ft.

The situation of the campsite was outrageously beautiful. A 100ft cascade behind the caravan would lull us into watery slumber, while a glacial-blue river rushed past the bottom of our bed. The mountain air was refreshingly cool. A gentle breeze felt like the caress of a newly starched and pressed pillowcase against my cheek. After weeks of 30°+, I inhaled greedily.

However, there is always a fly in the ointment. Excited about exploring the National Park, we discovered that dogs are not allowed off-lead *anywhere* in the Gran Paradiso. There were only four walks open to dogs and they were emphatically leads-on.

In the evening, it was more than just flies that sullied our balm. The campsite was mosquito city, so despite the challenging drive, we resolved to move on again the following day. In any case, the atmosphere in the campsite wasn't friendly. It reminded us of Sixt in our first year on the road. It was full of hoary, beardy types who have no truck with people avoiding the mosquitoes and character-forging hardships of proper mountain life by staying in a namby-pamby caravan. There were clearly no extra points to be gained for manoeuvring such a large and sissy caravan up a mountain.

Franco, the owner, was charming. He retained his

cool when we fused the electrics by switching on our water heater. Mark explained.

"It can't have fused the electric. It's on the lowest setting; 1KW!"

Franco nearly fainted.

"1KW! No wonder it fused. Why do you need a water heater anyway? There is free hot water in the building."

Franco had climbed Aconcagua and Mont Blanc. Maybe he had no truck with caravan-based softies either, although I doubt that many caravans made it to the campsite – certainly if they had any sense. We had passed road maintenance crews who were roped on and wearing climbing harnesses. I would definitely think twice about towing the road named SR23 again.

6

AGRICAMPEGGIO CORTE COMOTTO, VERONA, ITALY

Tea & Cake – but no Sandals – in the City of Romance

"Imposs-ee-billi."

It would have been rude not to drop into our spiritual home in Gressoney, Monte Rosa, en route to Verona. We had viewed a potential apartment for the winter ski season, which had a large parcel of land to the side. "Imposs-ee-billi" was the very Italian reaction to a commitment to pay a deposit straight away if we could leave our caravan parked in a discreet corner for the winter.

However, we departed the mountains no further forward in our quest for winter digs. We braved the toll roads, since all alternatives were tortuous mountain routes. This meant that we had just the three near-misses on the autoroute due to enterprising Italian driving.

In the interests of moderation, we try to drink

alcohol only at weekends. However, when we arrived at our campsite, the stress of the journey was not the only reason for our transgression. The balmy warmth and the full moon hanging in a pastel-pink sky just demanded that a bottle of red be broached.

9pm and I was still outside in a bikini, listening to cicadas. As we relaxed on the tranquil lawn in front of our pitch, we could admire the vines growing opposite, while the dogs chased joyfully around. We had struggled to find any campsites near Verona, other than those around the Italian lakes. It was peak season, so we knew that these would be rammed and costly; upwards of €40 per night. Then we found Agricampeggio Corte Comotto, a small site just three miles from Verona. Pitches cost less than €20 per night and it was obviously run with the utmost love and care.

The railway station was a short walk from the campsite but dogs were charged at half-fare and had to wear muzzles. Since only one dog per passenger was allowed, we would drive into Verona.

Our first visit to Verona had been for our first wedding anniversary. We are not towny folk, but we adore her compact charm. Before we even arrived, the first glimpse of the golden buildings of 'The City of Romance' lining the banks of the River Adige made me realise how much I had missed her. Twenty years is too long to be parted from a beloved.

By mid-morning, the temperature had reached 41°C but we strolled into Verona following a route of delicious cool, through narrow streets kept in permanent shade by the shuttered facades of soaring, Renaissance buildings. Our route smelled of moss and ancient, musty mortar. I was on a mission to find replacement sandals, since my utility sandals had broken on a steep and inappropriate climb in Monte Rosa – and my flip flops had not been seen since the Auvergne.

Needless to say, many of the shops on Verona's main shopping streets were closed for a couple of hours. It was that most important of Italian times: *pranzo*, or lunch. Sometimes you will find that even the restaurants in Italy close for lunch. If you question this, you will be met with incredulity.

"But when will the staff eat?"

We treated ourselves to a pizza in Piazza Erbe, under our namesake, the Torre dei Lamberti – Lambert's Tower. Built in 1172, it is the tallest tower in Verona. Our waiter, Alex, enticed us in by promising "Free drinks for the dogs!" Less than €10 later, we had enjoyed a delicious pizza in the centre of a World Heritage city, with free entertainment from Alex and his sidekick, who engaged in good-natured fun and banter with their customers.

In Piazza Bra, outside Verona's famous Roman Arena, we had arranged to meet two dear friends, Stefano and Roberto. A rendezvous in a foreign city felt exotic and jet-set. It would have been romantic to enjoy our coffee and cake at the tables on the pavement, outside the old fashioned *pasticceria*. However, the heat forced us to succumb to the lure of air conditioning. The genteel interior was all cool, mint-green tiles, chandeliers and dark, aged wood – and the management didn't bat an eyelid about welcoming four dogs.

"I want some shoes that are a cross between sandals and hiking boots." I announced to Stefano. He nearly choked.

"And you are looking for those in *Verona*?!"

It was a big ask.

Later, on marble flagstones, we passed the designer emporia of Via Mazzini. We have been 'away from it all' for a few years now. The only aromas that have assaulted our nostrils have been natural: herbs, hay, cut grass, pine and the fresh, clean air that you find in the mountains or by the sea. The manufactured scent of expensive perfumes was overpowering. It smelled as sickening and unnatural to me as the cloying, petro-chemical stench of an oil refinery.

"All this stuff we don't need!" I said to Mark as we passed window after window of expensive exclusivity. Hordes of tourists were tramping round, weighted down with logo-ed bags. I wondered if their excess of purchases would bring joy into their lives. I love the fact that there was nothing I wanted that could have made me any happier – except a new pair of outdoor sandals.

My recent full-scale loss on the sandal front had forced me into a pair of trainers. Not only were they uncomfortable in 40°C, but eclectic when paired with my summer dress on the chic streets of Verona.

On the up side, we did manage to score an Italian Pay-As-You-Go Data SIM card, which gave us 30GB of Data for €15 per month – twice the allowance of our badly-behaved UK SIM for the same price.

We reflected that while Italy may be famous for footwear, trying to buy utility sandals in Verona was...

"Imposs-ee-billi!"

...

Postscript:

A few months later, we investigated the possibility of renting the same apartment for the season without parking the caravan.

It was "Imposs-ee-billi!" because the owner had accepted a one-week booking at Christmas.

7

THREE CAMPSITES & A GRAVEYARD, VIPAVA, SLOVENIA

Dead Ends & Hidden Gems

"You can stay here if you want!" cackled the old woman, as she rearranged flowers on the grave.

We had reached a dead end; literally. Rather than our chosen campsite, the road petered out at a cemetery in Slovenia. Earlier, Mark had enthused,

"We can't miss it. I don't have the full address, but Vremski Britof is only a small village. I found the campsite on a blog. It sounds fab. Right by a river!"

Campsite Dujčeva Domačija was not listed in our satnav, but its postcode had led us confidently down the narrow road to the cemetery. It was the kind of narrow road that stirs one single emotion when you're towing a large caravan: "I hope that we won't need to turn around..."

Mark had asked if there was a campsite nearby. The lady looked amused as she gestured to indicate that the cemetery was the full extent of facilities. That was when she gave us a wicked grin and invited us to stay.

We weren't ready to repose with the deceased, so we executed a U-turn in the car park and beat a retreat.

"I saw a sign for another campsite, but the road was closed." I optimised – my very own verb for 'optimism to the point of stupidity'.

Things were getting fraught after a long and stressful journey. Our departure from Verona had been delayed. Unable to activate the Italian Data SIM card, Mark had popped back into the city to sort it out. A-roads would have doubled our journey time, although as we approached Trieste, we left the autoroute due to heavy traffic. We wanted to avoid entering Slovenia on a motorway anyhow; otherwise, we would have had to pay for a seven-day vignette to allow a short hop on the motorway.

Now, it was 6pm. Desperate to find a campsite before they all closed for the evening, Mark's executive decision was to take the road that was closed. We both prayed that the campsite was before the closure.

It wasn't, so we had to negotiate our substantial dimensions around a second 50-point turn.

A helpful local stopped his car and assured us that the campsite was definitely open. He gave us directions for a 12-mile diversion, which bypassed the road closure to approach from the opposite side of the river. Of course, by the second turn, we had forgotten the directions and were developing differing opinions as to the correct route. We pulled over before the differences became too radical and agreed that our best option would be to settle on a campsite for which we had proper directions. The satnav has thousands of camp-sites pre-programmed in and it gave us a list of those nearby. However, we had not appreciated that 'nearby' was as the crow flies.

It tempted us with campsites 'within 10km' of our current position, which were 30km away when we selected them. Many were back on the coast and cost upwards of €40 per night. Besides being expensive, they looked horribly commercial.

I Googled 'campsite' on my phone and discovered Kamp Vrhpolje.

"It's twelve miles away in Vipava. TripAdvisor says it's 'The best campsite in Slovenia'."

Since we had its address and it was listed in the satnav, we opted to go there. We arrived just before 7pm after a spectacular hairpin ascent and descent, plus a race with a bicycle. The cyclist was determined that we were not going to overtake him on the down-hill. He succeeded by an admirable margin.

With the onset of desperation, I had started to make mental notes of car parks and lay-bys where we might stop overnight if our mission failed. As the satnav led us straight past a miniscule, crowded camp-site with a tiny concrete bridge leading on to it, we were not brimming with confidence.

I walked over the dainty, arched bridge, which was perfectly proportioned to provide access for a gnome with a fishing rod. It looked distinctly less suitable for transporting several tons of caravan across a ditch.

"We are full."

My heart sank, although in truth, we were too large for the small field and Kismet would probably have rendered the local gnomes bridgeless.

The owner kindly gave me details of another two campsites in the area. Then, Mark and I delivered the greatest show on earth. We executed a U-turn directly in front of the campers, who had all settled down for the evening with their glasses of wine. We don't travel inconspicuously: four dogs, a large caravan and a blue van crowned with an array of surf boards.

We had a face-off with a tractor as the satnav suddenly changed its mind, so we got out of his way by performing our second U-turn. Then it decided that it was imperative for us to follow a tiny, narrow road. An oncoming local skidded his car sideways to block our route. He leaped out of his car and ran towards us, waving his arms.

"*Don't go up there!*"

We told him our destination and realised that the satnav must have been simply turning us around again. So, we performed a further U-turn to make our third pass of the campsite. Happy campers raised a glass to our progress.

"Cheers" I heard them call. Or maybe it was "Idiots!"

Choosing our third-time-lucky campsite by the 'pin-in-the-map' method, we wiggled up another precipitous set of hairpins to Kamp Tura. The last couple of bends were so steep that we were forced to execute them in first gear. Oil from Big Blue's exhaust sprayed liberally down Caravan Kismet's side while her clutch was starting to smell like an arson attack on Fort Dunlop. In its heyday. Before its transformation from tyre factory to Travelodge.

It was 8.30pm and our desperate search had occupied nearly three hours. Desolate, tired tears began to prick at my eyes as I wandered into reception. Impenetrable rows of vehicles packed side by side in the site had not escaped my notice.

A broad, friendly smile greeted me as Bojana, the owner, said that she would find us a place, even if we had to spend the first night in her car park.

"I never turn anyone away. Someone will leave tomorrow, so you will be able to move on to a pitch."

I felt like I had received a royal pardon on the scaffold.

Pitched on a piece of waste land at the end of the site, we even managed to connect to an electrical bollard. Our little plateau granted a spectacular view over the Vipava valley and its fabulous vineyards. Almost sheer rock walls of the Gradiska Tura soared above us. We had stumbled upon a hidden gem. Later, I discovered that Vipava had made the year's Top 10 in Lonely Planet's 'Best in Europe'.

With the unexpected additions to our journey, the pups had been cooped up in the van for eight hours. I took them for a leg-stretch and remarked that there were plenty of walks straight from the campsite – and that they were all very steeply uphill.

Bojana was especially interested in our lifestyle. She looked at my passport when I told her that we had retired.

"I'm only one year younger than you!" she exclaimed. However, the campsite was her own business. "I *love* my job," she told me.

"We used to get up at 4am to drive into work for a big corporation in London."

She agreed that our working lives differed markedly from her lot in the pure and picturesque mountains of Slovenia. Bojana was infectiously enthusiastic about Vipava and had co-authored a guidebook to the local area.

"You can visit Predjama, the castle in the cliff, Lipica and Ljubljana from here. Postonja caves are nearby, or Škocjan, which I think are even better. The dogs can't go inside the caves, but Postonja has kennels – and dogs can walk around the Škocjan cave park. I can arrange wine tours, rock climbing and show you all the best walking routes."

I thanked Bojana and bought some cold beers. We had earned them. They tasted like nectar.

As Mark and I sipped them in the gentle night, we agreed that, while it was against our philosophy of freedom and the ability to change our plans on a whim, there could be occasions in future where it might be prudent to make a campsite reservation, particularly in high season, on sites close to a multitude of popular tourist attractions.

With Kamp Tura, we had struck gold and would stay a while. Since we would have the same address for a bit, I checked out something important on the internet. The Sandals of my Dreams, delivered to Slovenia, would cost €110. The same pair was available in the UK for the equivalent of €68.

My chances of achieving a reasonably-priced pair of walking sandals had never seemed so remote.

8

HUNTING DRAGONS: BAREFOOT IN DOG-FRIENDLY LJUBLJANA, SLOVENIA

A Tale of Two Earthquakes & Sandal Success

Bojana had promised us a proper pitch when someone moved, but it was on a first-come-first-served basis. The campsite was full and vacant pitches disappeared immediately.

Following our three-campsites-and-a-graveyard epic, we didn't arise until 11.30am. Realising the stiff competition for pitches, we rushed to move the caravan before breakfast.

Rather than going through the fandangle of hitching her up, we moved house by pushing Kismet up the road. "Don't you have a motor mover?" the usual question rang out from a number of English couples who lined our route.

To save both weight and our leisure battery, we elected not to have a motor mover, a gadget which would position Kismet by remote control. With such a large caravan, many caravanners find this odd, however, they received our stock answer: "No. He's confident in his reversing!"

After two years of almost full-time touring, we have a well-honed system for setting up; a system from which we should know better than to deviate, even when moving just a short distance. We shoved Kismet into her new pitch but accidentally positioned her too close to a hedge, so we couldn't access the gas locker and water points. Once in position, she refused to budge by muscle power alone, so in the end we had to hitch her up anyway.

Rosie loves to find herself little caves to hide away. I'm ashamed to say that we didn't realise that she had sought refuge from the smouldering midday sun beneath the caravan. Thankfully she was not crushed when we towed Kismet forwards a few feet, although she did look shocked as she shot out from her shady den. To keep the fridge cold, we had connected up the electric immediately. As we drew Kismet forward, the cable caught under her wheel and nearly tore out the fitting.

Our English neighbours, Maureen, Jim and their dog Buddy had adopted a similar lifestyle to us. They had bought their first caravan as soon as they retired and were Living the Dream by spending a year touring. They were heading for Greece. Friends of theirs had travelled in Montenegro and Bosnia the previous year, so we picked their brains.

"UK insurance companies won't cover you, so you

have to buy insurance at the border. Our mates were a bit scared when the authorities took away their passports, but they were given back with the insurance."

Maureen and I agreed that caravans are like the Bermuda Triangle.

"I've lost a twenty-one-inch, deep-sided frying pan in ours!" she exclaimed.

This was even more impressive than my stealth-camouflaged (black) flip flops, which could have slipped into any corner of the caravan, although I suspected that they were holidaying together in the Auvergne.

The following day, with Ljubljana in our sights, we turned right at Vipava and climbed. Big Blue zig-zagged up to Col through magical scenery, with views back to the Nanos plateau. Regiments of green hills marched one after the other into the distance. Villages of terracotta-roofed white houses interspersed the zesty green. Vibrant red geraniums cascaded from window boxes overlooking pristine gardens. Slovenia is a beguiling country, with a bright, new feel; a marked contrast with the dilapidated, flaking stucco of run-down, rural villages in France or Italy.

Our entrance into the city of Ljubljana was by no means as picturesque as our approach to Verona, however. Modern office blocks and concrete walls covered with graffiti led us in. We parked a short walk from the centre in an open-air car park that cost just €6 for the day.

However, first impressions are only that. We

quickly realised that Ljubljana is our kind of town. One of the smallest capital cities in Europe, it is clean, relaxed and the pedestrianised centre is perfect for a quiet meander. The mix of styles among the imposing, colourful facades tells the tale of two earthquakes, as well as that of Slovenia's most celebrated architect. The ornate Baroque buildings reflect the rise in wealth and power of the Habsburg Empire after the city was almost levelled by a quake in 1511. Reconstruction following Earthquake II – The Sequel in 1895 resulted in the erection of more than four hundred Viennese Secessionist (Art Nouveau) buildings.

Post WWI, after the Habsburgs were deposed, Jože Plečnik, 'the harbinger of Postmodernism', shaped the city with his own take on urban planning. Plečnik's Ljubljana includes the marketplace, iconic buildings such as the National University Library, plus parks, plazas and the city's distinctive bridges and riverside embankments.

The city is cradled in a bend of the River Ljubljanica and overlooked by a magnificent, 12th-century hilltop castle. Not only that, we noted that it was twenty minutes' drive from ski resorts in the Slovenian Alps and 45 minutes from the Adriatic beaches for windsurfing. Our kind of town indeed!

Our city tour was based not on the historic sights, but on sports shops which might stock utility sandals. My feet were still obliged to endure steamy, summer temperatures in my only remaining choices of footwear – trainers or hiking boots.

We ambled along the river to Plečnik's Dragon Bridge, which is the symbol of Ljubljana. I do love a dragon. I was born in the Chinese Year of the Dragon and went to university in the country of the dragon, Wales. I studied martial arts and have always been fascinated by the fabulous Chinese and Japanese dragon dances. (I once read that the dance ends with the dragon pouncing on a ceremonial cabbage. I am not quite sure why...)

The sports shop near the Dragon Bridge yielded no sandals. After moseying some more, we stopped for a coffee in the shade, overlooking the bejewelled green river. A few SUPs passed. Our SUPs were on Big Blue's roof but our paddles were holding up the ceiling of our caravan awning. We cursed ourselves. A river trip would have been a wonderful way to see Ljubljana.

Sweltering summer temperatures were intensified by the city. The dogs sought out fountains to cool themselves. In a country famed for its majestic Lipizzaner horses, my favourite fountain was decorated with little, fat, bronze Thelwell-style ponies. Another, which allegedly mimicked Ljubljana's weather, sprinkled a fine mist over tourists. It was most welcome and refreshing in the heat – as was the enormous Nutella ice cream from a stall nearby.

Mark sealed his image as an English eccentric by walking barefoot around the city so that he could sense whether or not the pavements were too hot for our puppy-dogs' paddy paws.

Ljubljana was very dog-friendly. Technically, dogs

are supposed to be on leads in the Tivoli and Castle gardens; however, a printed leaflet in the tourist office intimated that, although leads were the rule, officialdom was inclined to overlook well-behaved dogs running free. The Fab Four were welcome in nearly all of the shops that we visited, including Lush. The girls made a huge fuss of them as we treated ourselves to a weight-saving, environmentally-friendly, solid shampoo-and-conditioner bar, whose delicious jasmine scent fragranced Caravan Kismet for the rest of our trip.

A capital city often reflects the character of its country's people. Ljubljana was happy, welcoming and laid back.

In stark contrast, InterSport Ljubljana did not welcome dogs and as far as I could tell, felt much the same about customers. They had a vast array of both shop assistants and sandals, but I still had to ask a sullen girl to help me to find the correct size and provide a left shoe. The sullen girl summoned a moody teenager, who told me that I must find my own left shoe from somewhere in the pile of boxes beside me and that the shoe in my hand was the right size.

"Stupid," he added. Although not out loud.

I requested another style in my size. He grumbled something; they didn't have it or he couldn't be bothered to look.

"Any other colours?"

"No."

Normally, I would have no truck with such an

establishment and would have left immediately. However, toasting tootsies forced me to abandon all principles regarding customer service. Unlike the staff, my new pair of Tevas was comfortable and supportive. And, a bit like the service, they were reduced by 30 per cent.

9

WAGGY TAILS & WHITE HORSES: A TRIP TO THE FAMOUS STUD FARM AT LIPICA, SLOVENIA

Dobrodošli Dogs

My first love – before Freddie Mercury; even before Mr Spock; before pretty much anything else that I can remember other than my family – was horses.

Today, I would fulfil a dream. Mark had considered it as a surprise for my 40th birthday, but the place was closed. Last year, we had been forced to bail out of a planned trip due to violent thunderstorms. Third time lucky, we were going to visit the famous stud at Lipica (Lipizza in Italian) where they breed the iconic white Lipizzaner dressage horses used by the Spanish Riding School in Vienna.

As youngster, I would not miss the TV show *The White Horses*, the Lipizzaner-based adventures of Julia and Uncle Dmitri. The theme tune to the show was performed by the artist *Jacky*. On the radio, it was always introduced as, 'It's Jacky and her White Horses'. At the age of four, I wasn't sure how Mum and Dad had done it, but every time it was played, I was sure that it had been requested especially for me.

The drive from Kamp Tura to Lipica was breathtaking: gorgeous countryside and scented meadows which, in typical Slovenian style, were all as perfect and neatly kept as a prize-winning garden at the Chelsea Flower Show. I felt blessed as we drove into the stud at Lipica to be greeted by a herd of mares and foals; a welcoming committee, they galloped up to the fence. Mark stopped for me to get out and pet them. The foals came to nuzzle at me. A cyclist halted next to me.

"These are very special horses," he said.

Then the herd thundered off. That made my day – and we had not even reached the entrance.

Buying a ticket was a pleasure; the service was welcoming and unhurried. The options were to look around the stud or to include admission to a daily show. Depending on the day, the show would be either a training session or a full-on presentation of *haute école* (high school) classical dressage. If you have not seen it before, I strongly recommend the dressage. It is truly amazing to see these majestic horses put through their paces. Armed with the show times and directions to the training hall, we entered the world's oldest continuously operating stud, whose history dates back to the 1500s.

Besides dressage, Lipizzaners are used as carriage horses. I petted a coach-and-two waiting at the gate. The velvety muzzle of the nearside horse pushed into my hands as he leaned against me, ever so gently.

The beautifully kept, sweeping, emerald-green pastures were dotted with shady trees, edged with painted white fences and criss-crossed with wide carriage-ways linking the stud to Vienna and Trieste. Even without the horses, Lipica would be a fabulous place to visit.

Having seen a Lipizzaner dressage show before, I had chosen to see the horses training. I was intrigued to observe how the horses were worked, to develop them to such an incredible standard. Dogs could roam everywhere in the stud except the inside the training hall, so Mark whisked away the pups while I watched the show. In my absence, The Fab Four bonded with a little black foal and a lady groom invited everyone into her stable yard for a drink and a cooling douse with a hosepipe.

As the huge double doors of the training hall opened, I saw the shadow of a magnificent horse projected on to one of them, moments before four elegant, muscular white stallions tiptoed into the arena. Three were being ridden, while one, seven-year-old Maestoso Navarra, was worked 'in hand'. He was learning the 'Capriole' – known as one of the 'Airs Above the Ground'. The Capriole requires the horse to leap high into the air and kick out with its back legs.

Seeing it in training showed how difficult it was for the horse. Maestoso Navarra could achieve little leaps and little kicks, but could not manage both together. The finished move is carried out six feet in the air – at the head height of a man.

The horses were given plenty of love and praise; they were clearly cherished and trained by kindness. Only stallions are strong enough to perform high school dressage. Mares and stallions with no aptitude for dressage are ridden or used to pull carriages.

However, this style of dressage was not developed just for show. The origin of such horsemanship was on the battlefield. The Capriole is a manoeuvre designed to clear space when crowded in. It would be a brave man indeed who remained standing in front of a ton of leaping horse or held his ground behind as a pair of iron-shod hooves lashed viciously at his head.

From the front row, I watched the horses perform movements such as the diagonal half pass at trot and canter, circles and pirouettes. Maestoso Navarra did some mounted work after his Capriole training. The hoof beats shook the floor and I was moved to tears to see such powerful animals curving their necks to obey the gentle pressure of the bit. Snorting and frothing at the mouth, they showed such restraint and control, moving as precisely and delicately as ballerinas.

Boris, our host, commentated in five languages: Slovenian, English, French, German and Italian. With three of these a work in progress for me, it was surprisingly good practice. The choice of music to accompany the show was eclectic – 'La Vida Loca', 'Gimme, Gimme, Gimme (a Man after Midnight)' and 'Ring of Fire' – although La Vida Loca had a particularly good beat for dressage.

After the show, I re-joined Mark and the pack for the guided tour around the stables. Lipica takes its name from the linden trees found in the village. I have always thought that Lipizzaners resemble the noble Spanish Andalusian horses. Evidently, the six founding stallions of the Lipizzaner breed were mostly of Andalusian origin, along with one Arabian. Crossed with the local Karst heavy horses, the breeding produced a lighter but still very powerful animal.

We met Conversano Bonadea, the black stallion. It is a tradition for the stud to keep one black stallion and one bay mare. Lipizzaners used to come in all colours, including piebald (black and white) and skewbald (brown and white) but the Habsburgs, who founded the stud, favoured the grey, so now most Lipizzaners are grey. In equestrian terms, there is no such thing as a white horse. Even the purest white is termed grey. Lipizzaner foals are born black or bay (bay is a brown coat with black "points" i.e. legs, mane and tail.) The horses turn grey as they mature, between the ages of six to ten years.

The stone walls of the Old Stables were 5ft thick. Inside, the temperature remains constant and despite the heat of the day, it was delightfully cool. Swallows nesting in the rafters whistled and swooped around our heads as we met the blue-blooded occupants.

From a shady table under the trees, we had lunch at the calm and relaxing Karst restaurant. The Fab Four went down a storm with staff and guests. From the guide to the waitress, everyone showed incredible pride in both the stud and their country. They went out of their way to ensure that we got the very best from our day. *Dobrodošli* is the Serbo Croat word for 'Welcome' – something that you will experience to the full in Slovenia.

When we returned to see him, the little black foal came once again to be petted. A small girl, who reminded me of my younger self, stroked him as he poked his nose through the fence. She lit up as she put her hands to her nose and sucked in a deep breath, savouring that wonderful, sweet smell of horse. As a child, I remember doing exactly the same – and irritating Mum by refusing to wash my hands for hours, because I loved the scent so much.

At 5pm, the herds of mares and foals are brought galloping back from the fields, but since we were tired and the dogs were hot, we set off home early. It was an excellent choice – we had barely cleared the gates when the sky turned indigo and an immense lightning bolt slashed the sky. Rain blowing in through Big Blue's wide-open windows was a welcome relief from the heat.

Climbing the steep turns back to Kamp Tura, we realised that we might not have made it up in the wet with Caravan Kismet in tow. Big Blue lost traction on the steeper sections, even without Kismet's 1.5T dead weight pulling her backwards.

A contented snooze when we got back completed a perfectly magical day out.

10

KAMP OTOČEC, SLOVENIA

Camping & Castles on the River Krka

Our only job was to take down the awning, but it took a while to get on our way from Kamp Tura. Everyone seemed to stop and chat, not that we were complaining. It's all part of the fun.

I took the pups up the hill for their morning walk through the cool, leafy woodland. After the initial steep climb, there was a long, almost level path through the trees. If you're into rock-climbing, there is a plethora of routes, varying from Grade 3 (novice) and 7c+ (super-expert). A one-hour ascent to the summit of Gradiška Tura has a Via Ferrata (protected rock-climbing route) at the top for the bold – and properly equipped.

A Dutch couple showed us a picture of 'The Eye', a hole in the rock above Ajdovščina, featured in Bojana's guide book. There was no doubt. We would have to come back.

Mark had plotted a scenic drive to our next destination, which was shorter than the route proposed by the satnav. The landscape was glorious. Mark commented that Slovenia reminded him of a golf course. It looks natural but manicured. Everywhere is tended and cared for. Even the roadside verges are neat. Forested hills, vineyards and meadows, as green as any you would find in Surrey, are replete with colourful flowers. Every village is pristine and tidy. It was so perfect; it could have been 'Theme Park Slovenia'.

A brief, but massive thunderstorm broke out. Once again, we were relieved as it misted our skin through the open windows. The sudden, torrential rain awakened the dusty scent of the road, along with fresh grass and wild herbs. Back in the sunshine, we passed a field full of black-and-white storks. Hilltop villages of white houses with bright, terracotta roofs and spired churches punctuated our route. Nearing Krka, Alpine-style chalets with long, narrow plots and vineyards striped the hillsides.

We tour with a refillable, LPG gas cylinder. Although we did find one garage that sold LPG, our adapter seemed to be just ever-so-slightly the wrong size. It was not the end of the world, but would preclude our going off-grid. Our cylinder contained enough gas for cooking, but not enough to power the fridge for a week in 30°C.

Just after the Alpine chalets, we drove into a

phantom menace. The road was dead straight and bordered by a spookily dark forest. Shadowy limbs of skeletal trees arched to meet over our heads, giving the feeling of driving into a tunnel. The carefree, summer sky turned inky black and ahead was a blurry interface; it looked like a time-slip in a film.

Big Blue hit the weather front head-on and we felt the jolt as she punched through the pressure wave. Inside was a strange, monochrome world. Trees rustled and moaned like banshees, while fallen leaves would suddenly lift and swirl, or chase in a mad hunt past our windows. As windsurfers, we have felt many weather fronts – and ridden the winds that they suddenly generate with unfettered joy – but this was the first time that we had been able to see one.

Kamp Otočec was in an idyllic location. Right on the bank of the River Krka, we pitched overlooking a lush, green island and its gothic castle, Grad Otočec. The only water castle in Slovenia, it is now a luxury hotel.

Our entrance, however, was somewhat nerve-wracking. First, we had to turn Big Blue and Kismet sideways on to the now howling wind (Bojana had warned us about the Bora, a wind notorious for whipping up suddenly and ferociously.) Then, we had to cross the River Krka via two wooden bridges, each with a 3T weight limit. Laden, we suspected that Big Blue weighed more than 3T – and that was without Kismet's 1.5T in tow.

We stopped to contemplate our options.

"I don't think there's any way around."

"I've just seen three cars on the bridge at once. They must weigh more than 3T."

As we took a run at it, I invoked the intervention of the gods.

"Don't collapse. *Please don't collapse...*"

Later, from the waterside, I watched two swans sprint up the river to take off while storks flapped lazily past our windows. It was magical – but that was no different from the rest of Slovenia.

Ruby loves water. Once we were settled, she spent seven hours paddling. Everybody was in their element. There were butterflies, mayflies, rudd and other tiny fish to watch in the shallows. The water and sky were alive with birds. Our outlook was across the unhurried river, which slipped languorously past the fresh, green island, from whose banks the branches of weeping willows kissed the water.

New neighbours arrived. Charlotte and Didier from Belgium joined us for tea with their nine-month old red Cavalier, Oskar. Their ingenious micro-caravan next to Kismet was like Little and Large.

Reluctantly, Ruby allowed us to drag her away from the water to explore the woodland beyond the castle, whose walls and turrets were mirrored perfectly in the calm water. Crossing a field, we met our first Roma gypsies, dining al fresco in family groups. One chap was roasting at least ten chickens on a spit over a fire. A few children approached and asked for money, although they went away as soon as we refused. We kept our Fur Babies close. The kids were incredibly quick on the uptake; as we recalled Lani, our cute, little black baby, they immediately started calling her by name.

That night, we expected to hear the Roma. Ten chickens suggested that quite an event was in the offing. We didn't hear a peep.

The following day, Didier and Charlotte set off walking the same route, intent on reaching the main town. They soon returned; much of the route was on the road and it was too hot, particularly for Oskar. They told us that the Roma were out in force on the field and were spit-roasting a whole pig.

A cool-down in the Krka seemed in order. Mark set out for a SUP test run, but the pack got frantic. Mark didn't hear my shouts for him to come back and landed over on the island. Lani, not usually a swimmer, set off single-mindedly after him. I rushed in to swim after her. Although the current in the middle was fairly slack, she is tiny and I was afraid that she might be swept away.

Kai and Rosie followed me, leaving a distraught Ruby yelping on the shore. Princess can swim, but is too regal to condescend to such base activities voluntarily. Once we all landed on the island, I held the pooches as Mark returned to shore, collected Ruby, my SUP and the doggie life jackets, then paddled back to re-unite everybody on the island.

Organised at last, we went for a little tour. The river was very shallow in places but was great fun to explore. Of course, Mark had to run the rapids and everyone fell off, but the rapids were not the scariest part of the day. A SUP-eye view of the wooden bridge that we had crossed with the caravan struck fear into our hearts. The number of cracked and broken timbers suggested that an alternative departure route would not only be wise, but essential.

Oskar and Didier took to SUPing like naturals. Oskar has his own Instagram account and insisted on a photograph to post with his new friends – five pups on SUPs. A lady was paddling around with a Springer Spaniel in a Canadian canoe. It just shows, there are many ways to float a Fido.

A German couple next door had toured Romania the previous year. Following the horror stories that we had been fed about Romania, we were still extremely nervous about going there. They told us:

"Romania? It's fairy-tale…"

"What about the packs of throat-tearing hounds?"

"What? All the stray dogs that we met just wanted affection. They slept under our camper!"

We felt slightly reassured, although I had still had a cunning Romania Research plan up my sleeve. I had received a message on Facebook from Andrew and Sharon, a British couple Living their Dreams by running a campsite in Hungary. They said, "Don't forget to pop in and see us at Tranquil Pines. We are very dog-friendly, with miles of forest tracks behind us for walking." There was a promise of complementary cold beers, but I also thought that Andrew might be able to provide local knowledge regarding the wisdom, or otherwise, of taking a caravan and four dogs into Romania.

11

TRANQUIL PINES CAMPING, KOPPANYSZANTO, HUNGARY

Brushes with the Law, The Kings of Cool & Communism

We pushed on towards Romania, carefully avoiding the bridge as we left Otočec. Impressive Alpine panoramas and delightful hill villages were scattered along our route as we wound out of Slovenia on A-roads. Croatia could not have been more different. On the border, the landscape immediately flattened into acres of scrub land, fronting the dull, grey skyscrapers of Zagreb.

An instant positive in Croatia, however, was a garage that sold LPG. These had been rare in Slovenia; we had found only two and had been thwarted by one dodgy adapter and a refusal. Not all forecourts countenance the refilling of gas cylinders. Re-charging is dangerous unless, like ours, the cylinder is designed to be refilled. Making our way to less-developed countries, we had concerns about maintaining our LPG supply. Later, we discovered that LPG was available at virtually every street corner in Hungary and Romania.

The toll road did get prettier as we drove east, but it became very mountainous. A four-hour hop on the motorway seemed preferable to the more scenic, nine-hour alternative.

En route, we had a few worrying brushes with the law. A sombre policeman on a motorbike, like Robocop behind his dark shades, flagged us over to the hard shoulder. Our stomachs churned as we slowed to a halt. Rumours of foreign vehicles being targeted for large, on-the-spot fines flashed through our minds. What on earth had we done wrong?

He sailed past and continued on his way. Relief flooded through Big Blue. It was simply a heavy-handed tactic to allow clear passage for a prison bus and its escort.

At the Hungarian border, we had to produce everything: passports, driving licences and ownership documents for both the van and caravan. Although I had reclaimed custody of all documentation, including the Mont Blanc tunnel pass, it still didn't go well.

"This is a problem!"

A granite-faced border guard asked us to step out of the cab and shook Mark's photo-card driving licence in our faces.

Uncomprehending, we pointed out the permissions and explained at length that Mark had a lorry licence and was perfectly entitled to tow the caravan. The policeman flicked the licence dismissively and jabbed at the date. We realised in horror that Mark's photo-card had expired.

"Five hundred kuna fine in Croatia!" he barked.

"The licence hasn't expired, only the card..."

Silently, we admonished ourselves. Only stupid people don't check their documents before they travel.

I produced my licence, "I can drive!"

He didn't even try to disguise his look of disdain. The policeman turned to Mark. His prodding finger almost penetrated Mark's shoulder.

"You drive!"

Then he turned his back and stalked off.

A man with a suspicious licence versus a woman towing a caravan legally. Clearly a no-brainer. He waved us on our way.

At the motorway toll station in Hungary, an epic sign-language conversation took place. I discovered through a lengthy mime with the non-English speaking attendant that in many European countries, vehicles and trailers are registered separately. In Hungary, each requires a vignette. Big Blue and Kismet sharing the same registration number prompted confusion and disbelief. However, this was as nothing to the incredulity when I cancelled the transaction the second after I had paid for it, because I realised that the non-motorway route was only thirty minutes longer and would save us €38.

Hungary was flat and featureless until we reached the shores of Lake Balaton, landlocked Hungary's 'seaside'. Even though it rarely gets more than 14mph of wind, we thought that it might provide some wobbling possibilities for our windsurfers.

The coolest place on earth is Paia on Maui's North Shore. Mark had taken me there to windsurf for my Hawai'i Five-O (fiftieth) birthday. In Paia, everyone is a dude with sun-bleached locks and a surf board under their arm. In contrast, at Lake Balaton, everyone was pasty white with a pot-belly and a brightly-coloured inflatable under their arm.

At the end of the lake, past a shoreline fringed with concrete holiday villages that could pass for prison camps, we turned right towards Tranquil Pines. The road was deceptive; it looked smooth, although Big Blue and Kismet rode up it like a pair of trawlers playing tag on stormy seas. We guessed that the surface underneath was either cobbled or subsiding. The best ploy was to drive slowly in the middle of the road. This worked really well until you met a Hungarian driver doing the same in the opposite direction. Except that Hungarians don't do 'slow'.

It was a relief to arrive safely at Tranquil Pines. We passed a lot of long, low, Roma houses, each with its own small parcel of land. The people were obviously poor. Several of the houses had partially collapsed. Nevertheless, we got smiles and a cheery wave as we passed. Hungary was a Big Brother communist state until 1989, although the Soviet Military didn't leave finally until 1991. Later that evening, Andrew told us:

"During communism, my neighbour's house had a radio built into the wall. It couldn't be switched off; it spouted Russian propaganda 24-hours a day. Once, he made a comment to the wrong person and landed his whole family in prison for a month."

That cold beer was waiting and, after a long drive in 30°C+ heat, it was most welcome. Rather than cook, we treated ourselves to Andrew and Sharon's speciality, home-made goulash. It was the best I have ever tasted. Smoky and rich, it had been slow-cooked over an open fire for five hours.

Being so far off the beaten track, our fellow guests were all intrepid travellers. Two couples had just passed through Romania, so we shared stories and beer late into the night. They told us that Romania was beautiful and the people were lovely. We felt slightly reassured, despite reading about one Romanian camp-site whose owners advised guests to remain in their vehicles from 9pm to avoid attack. At 9pm, they released their massive dogs to keep the bears and wolves at bay.

It promised to be an interesting trip.

12

CAMPSITE ROUTE ROEMENIË, MINIŞ

Paradise Found or Hell on Earth? We Discover 'The Voice of Reason' & The Roots of Romania's Canine Catastrophe

At Camping Motel Makó, right on the Hungarian border with Romania, we considered what we were about to do.

Mark and I have travelled extensively in what you might call 'challenging' countries – across South America, Africa and Asia. Yet we had never worked ourselves into such a frenzy of doubt about visiting anywhere as we had with Romania. Before we set off, no-one had a good word to say about Romania and our research had thrown up all kinds of horror stories about packs of wild dogs; bears; wolves; pickpockets; scammers; and officials who like a bribe. We read that the going rate for a bribe was €100 – but increased in life-threatening situations. "It's against the law to give animals water," said one Romanian blogger. "They beat dogs and leave out poison to kill strays." "Dreadful roads, terrible driving, drunken truckers..." And as for Roma gypsies: "They slashed open my handbag... They'll have the glasses off your face!"

That spring, Romania had suffered torrential rain and floods. Today, the day before we were due to cross the border, reports filled the press of anti-government riots in Bucharest and most other major cities.

We emailed the Romanian tourist board in London. Their inbox was full. We contacted their office in Bucharest. They did not reply.

We checked with the British and US Consulate websites. Despite the rioting, both said Romania was safe.

So often, the solution is right under your nose. I realised that I had completely overlooked the most golden of opportunities. My friend Lia had lived in the UK for so long that I had all but forgotten that she is Romanian. I emailed her and soon, my very own, personal 'Voice of Reason', duly confirmed:

"LOL about that blog! It is not against the law to give animals water. What a stupid thing to say. Lots of people have dogs as pets... I had no idea there was a going rate *(for bribes)*. Giving and receiving a bribe is illegal so never, ever offer one. I'm not sure what life-threatening situations you are planning to get yourself into but most parts of Romania are safer than many parts of London!"

I used to live in Lambeth. I believed her.

"Take an umbrella and possibly a boat. They have had a true British summer so far with lots of rain and flooding. Oh, and beware of wild animals if you set camp in the forest," she added. "Romania still has some real ones left..."

And so, we swallowed hard and went in. We intended to avoid wolves and bears – of both the human and animal kind. However, we got one the second we crossed the border.

As we pulled into a petrol station to buy our vignette, a weathered, toothless face leaned in through the open van window, waving a wad of cash.

"What currency you want and how much?" he barked.

We declined politely, closed the window and decided to switch on the aircon for the rest of the journey.

...

"To make your life easier, just say the French *merci* for 'thank you'." Lia had said. "It's used a lot in Romania – it's easier than *multumesc*. Don't worry, though, most young adults speak English well. You'll be fine!"

Although the pronunciation is different, the Romanian language shares some similarities with Italian. What have the Romans ever done for us? Like any good occupying force, 2000 years ago they came, they saw and they slaughtered Romania's locals. The word 'Romania' actually derives from the Latin 'Romanus' – meaning 'Roman'. Thus, despite Romania being adrift in a sea of Slavic languages, a Lancashire lass with a slight grasp of Italian could read and understand a few road signs. It was an immense relief after our attempts to decipher Hungarian. (Curiously, Hungarian is Finno-Ugric – related only to Finnish and Estonian.)

The landscape became immediately flat – really flat; pancake flat; flatter than anything I have ever seen, even in the expansively flat bits of America. As far as the eye could see, the tallest thing was a tree, or the endless march of pylons and industrial buildings. The towns that we drove through were amazing; poor houses with boarded up windows and crumbling walls sat next door to shameless exercises in ostentation: huge creations, four storeys high, with turrets, pillars and terraces, fronted by gilded, wrought-iron gates. We discovered later that these were Roma houses.

The DN7 took us all the way through Pecica and Arad. The road wasn't too bad, with the notable exception of a single level crossing, which was anything but level. It boasted a crater so huge that it was probably visible from the moon. The slowing traffic had formed its own tailback. There was plenty to see as we queued, however: the giant power transformers of a massive electricity substation, as well as numerous roadside stalls selling plastic water containers and garishly-painted garden gnomes.

I have never had the urge to buy a gnome on a journey, but such is the wonder of experiencing different cultures. Plastic water containers were a different matter, though. Ours had developed a leak from frequent shoving in and out of Big Blue and was held together with duct tape. If only we had bought currency from our toothless friend at the border, it could have been problem solved.

Transylvania means 'the land beyond the forest'. As a child, I thought that it was fictional. In my imagination, it was a dark, menacing, misty place, filled with forbidding, gothic castles and characters like Dracula, Frankenstein and the occasional hunchbacked butler called Igor.

In contrast, as we delved deeper into Transylvania, the countryside got prettier and lumpier. Bright fields of yellow sunflowers fringed our view of the Western Transylvanian mountains, which shone under a cornflower-blue sky.

We had a vague address for our campsite. That is, we knew that it was located in Baile Lipova, which we approached through a run-down town called Păuliş. Traumatised by the denied opportunity to replace our water container, Mark became heavily focussed on obtaining currency. As such, he opted to drive the caravan around the narrow streets of Păuliş in search of an ATM. Since ATM skimming had been flagged as a popular Romanian pastime, we had been advised to use only official ATMs at banks. Naturally, we didn't find an ATM, although we did manage to attract rather a lot of attention. The satnav tried to persuade us to go up a cinder road to reach our campsite. We overruled it. Thinking back, this affront was probably the point at which it started in earnest to plot our downfall.

Rather than using our stalwart, ACSI-listed campsites, we had discovered this particular camping ground on a Romanian website. As we pulled into the car park, we were faced with what I can only describe as 'Communist Butlins in the 1950s'. The view out of the campsite swept over a terrace of derelict, red brick houses, whose windows looked like empty eye sockets. For the first time, we saw stray dogs. Six dogs, with a puppy, sheltered in the scrubby, overgrown hedgerow that surrounded the houses.

The campsite itself boasted a gaudily-painted concrete swimming pool with stark, square, concrete buildings behind. We were directed to pitch on the concrete parking lot. The temperature was 36°C and with no shade at all, I could feel the concrete reflecting the sun's burning heat back onto my legs as I went to check in. There was no way that this surface would pass Mark's barefoot test for puppy paws. The proprietors were sweet, but spoke no English, Italian, French or German and the charge was a rather steep €17 per night. There was an ACSI-listed campsite six miles away, so with a good-natured wave, we left.

The satnav directed us to continue down the campsite road, which soon changed from tarmac to large cobbles, each the size of a baby's head. As the caravan bounced down the road, it was interesting to see the tumbledown, agricultural houses which lined each side. Typical Transylvanian houses seemed to be colourful, long, low bungalows, oriented in rows with the narrow end facing the road. High gates led into the yards between each pastel-painted building, joining them all in an impenetrable line. A thick, black spaghetti of tangled electric cables festooned the skyline of every street.

"I think this is going to end up being the cinder road."

"It doesn't matter," Mark reassured me. I mean, how bad could it be?

It was the Revenge of the Satnav. The potholed, cinder road could be tackled at speeds no greater than 5mph. Little did we realise that this would be excellent practice for what was to come.

...

The second campsite in Miniș, Campsite Route Roemenië, was run by a German family. They welcomed us warmly and we were allocated a pitch next to the owner, Paul's father. He and Paul work for a foundation which helps Romanian children. Most of the proceeds from the campsite go into the charity. We were impressed, although the grass and the shade were also a compelling reason to stay. Paul's dad had two little dogs, a Jack Russell terrier and a Jack/Yorkie cross – which I decided should be called a 'Jackie'.

As evening fell, the heat of the day didn't lessen. We pitched in no time and parked our chairs in the lengthening shadow of the caravan. Mark had nipped into the village and found an ATM, so we were sorted. We had currency, a vignette and something for dinner.

There were still lingering traces of doubt, though. Some of the cities in the news were on our itinerary. Never one to overreact, I emailed our 'Voice of Reason' about the riots. Lia replied:

"Chill, people! There weren't any riots, just anti-government demonstrations. In Sibiu, after the marches and demos, the protestors cleaned up the city centre on their way home."

So, all was quiet on the Romanian front.

...

At cock's crow, we got up to move on. The only trouble was that the cock crowed at 11:50am, so we stayed another day. A lengthy blast of Romanian folk music on someone's radio at 8am had woken us, although we had managed to go back to sleep. The symphony of barking dogs had lasted all night. It had been a reasonably comical doggie duet.

"Buff Buff" – "*Woo Woo*" – "Buff Buff" – "*Woo Woo*" – "Buff Buff" – "*Woo Woo...*"

Well, the first few hours were comical.

I wanted to find out more about Paul's work with Romanian families. I felt a little ashamed that before coming to Romania, we had been so concerned about the legendary stray dog problem that we hadn't really considered the plight of her people. Paul's father said,

"How can I get a new car when these people have nothing?"

We are dog lovers but in the short time that we had been in Romania, we had seen many more people than dogs suffering. Although this is the root cause, it is not covered by the press. If the people were fine, they could look after the dogs. The story behind the stray dog problem in Romania is not one of cruelty; it is one of human misery.

Following an earthquake in the 1970s, many Romanians were left homeless and unable to care for their pets. Add to that communist dictator Nicolae Ceaușescu's modernisation of Romania; his path to 'our golden, socialist future' included plans to bulldoze around 8,000 rural villages. Large numbers of people were forcibly relocated from the countryside to high-rise, city flats, leaving them no with option but to abandon their dogs. Romania is poor and neutering animals is costly, so these events initiated a problem that would only grow.

13

MINIȘ TO CAMP AUREL VLAICU

Rainbows in Romania

"It's the festival of St Mary," we were told.

Not the best day to travel, but we were packed and ready when we found out.

There used to be over 500,000 German settlers in this part of Romania. Johnny Weissmuller – five-times Olympic swimming champ, better known as 'Tarzan' – was a German ethnic, born in Timișoara.

German Saxons were settled in Transylvania by the King of Hungary in the 1100s with a mission to defend the borders of the empire. It is possible that this Saxon migration lends some truth to the story of the Pied Piper, as many of the settlers came from Hamelin, the town whose children the Piper stole. Geography sentenced Transylvania to a turbulent history. Caught on the frontier between two superpowers, the Austrian Habsburgs and the Ottoman Turks, with regular incursions from Tatars and Mongols, war has been an unremitting fact of life in Transylvania.

Despite having lived there for centuries, huge numbers of Romanian Germans left after WWII and still more followed after the fall of communism in 1989. Nevertheless, many do return for the festival on the 15th August. The Assumption of the Virgin Mary into Heaven is one of the most important Christian and Orthodox religious feast days and is a national holiday in both Romania and Germany.

As we drove through Lipova, a huge market was in full swing. I would have loved to look around, although it would have been impossible to park, even without a 23-foot caravan in tow. The scenery was pretty as we continued on the DN7 to Deva. The motorway was 'closed' (read 'unfinished' – we saw the actual point at which unsuspecting vehicles could have plunged dramatically off the end!).

The road surface deteriorated as we drove east. Signs everywhere announced EU investment. The infrastructure was certainly improving; much faster, it would seem, than the driving. Without frequent sharp braking, cars overtaking us blindly would have ploughed into oncoming traffic. When driving in Romania, looking behind is as important as looking forward. The driving style definitely hinted towards Romania's Italian ancestry.

...

Deva was dominated by a castle on the hill. We were dominated by concerns that the satnav wanted us to turn off the DN7. In the end, we thought that maybe it knew best, since the campsite was not marked on our map. It was programmed to 'Fastest Route' not 'Shortest Route' so we figured that it wouldn't do anything stupid, like taking us across a field.

Away from the main road, it was certainly an interesting drive. We passed through several exquisite villages, such as Harau, which has a lovely church. A more incongruous sight was the large and popular water park, complete with brightly coloured slides, plonked in the middle of a cow field. One turn went almost back on itself. Getting the caravan around that was a masterclass in manoeuvring.

The fields along the route were full of pear-shaped hay ricks. I hadn't seen a haystack for about forty-five years. The colour palette of the countryside was earthy; much darker than the brilliant green meadows of the Alps and Slovenia. The long ridges of hills looked mossy, while the hay ricks were a muddy brown, unlike the radiant blond haystacks which populated the halcyon, sun-tinged countryside of my childhood.

All the way along our route we could see traffic flashing past us on the DN7, which ran parallel to (and much more quickly than) our twisty-turny, potholed road. Then we joined a dirt track that took us, caravan and all, straight through the middle of a corn field. It spewed us out on to tarmac at the end, but the real irony was that when we reached our campsite in Aurel

Vlaicu, we were less than a quarter of a mile from the modern and beautifully metalled DN7 trunk road.

That said, our tribulations were not yet over. The campsite entrance was tiny, cutting between two white-washed buildings. The approach was a 90-degree turn from a narrow village road. Dennis, the proprietor, reassured us, "We've had much bigger rigs than you. Just take a wide swing."

We got in. Just. When he saw the photos on Face-book, our Italian friend Stefano described it perfectly as "A honeymoon fit!"

It was 39°C. Shortly after we had pitched, a little front brought wind and rain. We could have danced naked in it. It was the coolest we had felt for weeks.

Kismet's picture windows overlooked the brooding mountains of Transylvania, swathed in mist as two lightning storms competed with each other. Fluorescent bolts of lightning cracked the sky and stabbed the landscape ahead while, to our right, a magnificent double rainbow shone through the ethereal light.

We were now well into bear and vampire country, but all we had on our minds were Rainbows in Romania.

14

ROMANCED BY ROMANIA

What Has the Satnav Got Against the DN7?

Who let the cocks out?

It's official. Romania is an extremely noisy country. The previous day's dawn chorus of folk music was replaced with an array of creaky cockerels, dogs in a speed-barking competition and laughing ducks. After little sleep, we decided on a quiet day of laundry and shopping.

The mercury didn't quite achieve the 39°C of the day before, but the pups were still very hot. To cool Kai, we draped him in a damp towel, like a toga. "When in Rome..." he said, but we reminded him that it was Romania. A gentle breeze helped to keep the caravan to a reasonable temperature and dried our laundry in no time.

A grey-haired chap in homespun garments approached the low, chicken-wire fence that separated our caravan from the allotment next door. With a gappy grin, he handed us a bucket full of beautiful, home-grown tomatoes. They were delicious. Not perfectly red nor perfectly round, but ripened by the sun.They knew nothing of cold storage, insecticides – or, it seemed, artificial fertilisers. An interesting aroma was unleashed when he started watering his crops. We remained hopeful that our clean bedding would avoid a spraying with liquid manure.

Mark went shopping. It was a straight line to the Lidl supermarket on the DN7, yet the satnav attempted to take him through something that looked, he said, like a South African township. But Hell hath no fury like a satnav scorned. It decided that another field was a much better bet than the dastardly DN7. I did wonder what it had against the DN7; or had we somehow activated a 'Random Adventure' algorithm by accident? After this latest aberration, Mark christened the dastardly device 'Naffsat'.

However, Naffsat definitely had some serious adventure on the horizon. I was horrified when Mark showed me a picture of the Transfăgărășan. Also known as the DN7C, it was our route across the southern Carpathian Mountains.

Nearly 100 miles long, the Transfăgărășan was built by Ceaușescu in the 1970s to provide swift military access across the mountains; a precaution against Soviet invasion. It clambers to 6,742ft on what looks on the map like a nest of writhing vipers, then passes nearly 3,000ft through Romania's longest road tunnel.

The year before, we had towed Kismet from Italy into Slovenia on the Predel Pass. At 3,793ft, we had considered that an achievement. The altitude attained by the Transfăgărăşan is just 260ft shy of England's highest mountain, Scafell Pike, perched on top of Predel.

Caravan-hating Jeremy Clarkson, former presenter of the TV programme *Top Gear*, declared the Transfăgărăşan "The best road in the world".

Thus, it was in honour of Clarkson that we planned to drive over it with a caravan. We hoped that he would get stuck behind us.

...

The campsite at Aurel Vlaicu soon captured our hearts. It was very friendly, a perfect base for sightseeing, boasted delightful views and had a picturesque dog walk straight from the campsite. With a backdrop of the Carpathian Mountains, a stroll along a raised dyke took us through a rural idyll of fields, flowers and pretty farmhouses, complete with hay being pitchforked onto horse-drawn carts.

A bit of a Plane Jane, I noticed that an aeroplane sculpture graced the slip road from the DN7. Research revealed that the village, originally Binţinţi, had been re-named in 1927 because it was the birthplace of aviation pioneer, Aurel Vlaicu.

Vlaicu first built and flew a glider with his brother, Ion. He subsequently designed and built three self-powered planes – the world's first metal aircraft. They won international prizes and acclaim for being among the best flying machines of the time. Because of his careful research with scale models, Vlaicu's aircraft were highly unusual: they all flew successfully straight away, needing no modifications.

Sadly, Vlaicu's brilliance was short lived. He was killed in 1913 when his Vlaicu II crashed in an attempt to cross the Carpathians, before his Vlaicu III was completed. He was mourned as a hero. This man from humble beginnings, who helped to invent the future, is featured along with his plane on Romania's 50-lei banknote. June 17th is Romania's National Aviation Day, selected to commemorate the date of Vlaicu's first powered flight in 1910.

We just hoped that we would not emulate Vlaicu's fate when we attempted to cross the Carpathians with a caravan.

15

CORVIN CASTLE & LAKE TELIUC

Cavapoos & Castles

It was not the most successful sightseeing day ever.

Following another thunderstorm during the night, it was cloudy – and much cooler. Castelul Corvinilor, or Corvin Castle, beckoned. Sometimes called Hunyadi Castle after its builder, John Hunyadi (Ioan de Hunedoara), Corvin is the largest medieval castle in Transylvania and among the largest in Europe. Dubbed one of the seven wonders of Romania, we had been told, "It is not as historic as Deva castle, but much more impressive."

Since we're shallow, we opted for impressive.

The castle's home town of Hunedoara was horrible. As we drove past industrial estates and crumbling, concrete apartment blocks, all of a sudden, we caught a glimpse of a gothic spire, glinting on the skyline. Police directed traffic into the parking area and the toilet attendant guided us into our space. He grinned with delight and made a huge fuss of the dogs. He even kissed Rosie on the nose – so much for Romanians hating dogs.

I have never seen a more beautiful castle. A fairy-tale vision, its magnificent turrets soared skywards, topped with coloured tiles which shone in the sunshine like dragon scales. In the shade of a huge yew tree, we sat and admired it as we tucked into our first chimney cake, or kürtőskalács – a foot-long, hollow spiral of dough, spit-baked over charcoal and served warm, with a crisp encrustation of sugar and cinnamon. Yum!

Even at 10:30am, the queue for the castle was phenomenal. To save us from waiting fruitlessly in line for hours in full sun, I thought it wise to check; dogs were not allowed inside. The moat was closed off, so we couldn't walk around the perimeter either. Entry to the history and guilds museums was free and a lady attendant informed us that dogs could go inside both.

"Romanian dogs are not so well behaved," she told us. "We had a few 'accidents' so dogs are no longer allowed inside the castle."

Although there is no proof, it is alleged that Romania's most infamous son, one Vlad Țepeș (Vlad the Impaler – the inspiration for Dracula), was imprisoned for seven years in an underground cell beneath the castle. History tells us that John Hunyadi certainly clashed with the Dracula family. Hunyadi's invasion of Walachia resulted in the brutal murder of Drac's dad and eldest brother, after which he installed Vladislav II, Vlad's second cousin, to rule in their place.

While imprisoned, Vlad Tepes was reputedly forced to eat rats and was sent half mad by the screams of victims being eaten alive by wolves and bears in the adjacent 'Pit of Scythes'. Some believe that his experience at Corvin was the origin behind his bloodthirsty habits. Like a frustrated Naffsat, Vlad quietly plotted his revenge.

The attendant offered to look after the pups while we went into the castle – and promised not to steal them! We were intrigued; her job at the castle seemed to comprise of sitting on the steps outside in the sunshine, drinking coffee, smoking and being nice to visitors. The queue still looked about half a day long, however, so we gave up.

The Fab Four were hot, so we shot off to Lake Teliuc. We drove for miles around the lake, but could find no access to its shore. The lake shimmered emerald-green, although it was here that we first noticed a universal scourge of the Romanian countryside: piles of plastic litter. International companies seem to have spotted the opening of a new market, with no regard to the lack of refuse and recycling facilities. Not their problem, I guess, so long as they turn a profit.

We checked out Campsite Ledo on the shores of the lake. A Dutch guy in Miniș had described it as "noisy and popular with Romanians". A fleet of giant, swan-shaped pedalos on the waterfront told us everything that we needed to know.

All sightsee-d out, we limped home to indulge in our evening ritual: reclining in the shade of the fruit trees as the sun went down, each cuddling a puppy. I am Ruby's girl; I love the feel of her warm, velvety tummy against my skin or her cold, button nose pushed into my neck. Kai cuddled Mark, while The Terrible Two, Rosie and Lani, our pocket rocket, mooched about the enclosure that we had built, getting up to mischief and trying to escape.

This year's Cavapoo containment was a great improvement on the haphazard selection of bikes, plastic boxes, string and blankets that we had deployed last year. We had purchased 25m of plastic-mesh barrier fence from eBay, which was light and rolled up quite neatly. Rosie had tested it comprehensively by repeatedly approaching at full speed, then throwing her full weight sideways against it. In no time at all, we learned that we had to peg down the entire perimeter to prevent her from burrowing underneath.

As we relaxed that evening, we detected a hint of a pig grunting, along with guinea fowl and a sheep. We had not seen a single animal, in spite of the morning cacophony, and began to wonder whether the farmer was responsible for the repertoire of noises.

The only wildlife that we had seen had been in the caravan. Even with the insect nets firmly closed, every night the ceiling was black with bugs. Our second evening ritual, just before bed, was hoovering them all up.

16

DON'T MENTION THE... DACIAN RUINS

Plus Plums, Pálinka & Papanași

"Do you feel like a Dacian Ruin today?" I greeted my beloved.

Our special morning noise was "Werp, Werp, Werp, Werp, Werp," which we presumed was a chicken. It was a persistent chicken; its fanfare accompanied breakfast and continued well beyond morning coffee. This could be substantive proof for our theory that the farmer was making all the noises; we still hadn't seen a single creature and every animal sound seemed to have a slightly imperfect-yet-comic interpretation.

As we emerged from the caravan, the dogs bounded as a baying pack to greet a German chap from a campervan opposite. Mark and I followed on rapidly to apologise and were introduced to Stefan and Mihaela, his Romanian girlfriend. Stefan replied good naturedly.

"No problem. We were more worried when we arrived late last night and while we were pitching, all we could hear was Hitler!"

They had mentioned the War. We looked chastened as we explained that we had been watching the documentary *The World at War*, which we would never knowingly do within earshot of any German neighbours. When we had selected our evening's viewing at 9pm, we had been in Splendid Isolation, so we had not even closed the windows or roof vents. The particular irony was that we had reached the *'Hitler Years'* episode, which featured many excerpts from the Führer's speeches, blasted forth, full of zeal, ardour and volume.

Mihaela giggled. "We were concerned that we were going to wake up and find the campsite overrun with White Supremacists."

As we chatted, Mihaela and Stefan gave us their top Romanian recommendations;

- Don't drive at night; people don't use lights and there can be horse-drawn vehicles on the road.
- Visit the Voroseana Valley on the famous Transalpina mountain pass. Try traditional Romanian fare at Restaurant Hanul Haiducilor. Stefan spoke highly of their papanași; a traditional sweet comprising of a warm doughnut, served rather delightfully with its hole, plus sour cream

and sharp blueberry jam – to which we
would later become hopelessly addicted.

- Go to '20 Pizza' in Sibiu but *do not* take the
caravan into town.

- And the best recommendation ever:
purchase a Vodafone Pay-As-You-Go SIM to
get 150GB of data for around €15 per month.
Romania is justifiably proud of her 4G
network. Stefan confirmed that coverage
was significantly superior to that in East
Germany or the UK.

It was all added to our list. With around twenty-five
stops to go, our main concern now was that we would
run out of time.

...

As it happened, Mark did feel like a Dacian Ruin,
so we got on with 'doing' Romania.

The drive up to the Orăştie Mountains was
gorgeously scenic. Bubbling, white cumulus clouds
towered above the dusky peaks as we approached from
the flat, brown and green patchwork of fields that
formed the Transylvanian plateau. Our destination,
the Sebeş valley, boasted just the three Dacian
UNESCO World Heritage Sites. In case you have not
been introduced, the Dacians were a Thracian people
who inhabited the area until the first century AD.

(Thrace was formed from parts of modern Bulgaria, Turkey and Greece.)

Romania is not big on signage, so we couldn't find the first site at Căpâlna. That we had missed it was confirmed when we arrived at Costeşti, the location of the second. Although a country fair was in full swing, we managed to park. It was still sultry, despite the altitude, so the dogs hit the river to cool down. Somehow, we lost Kai's lead in the water. A footpath sign pointed back towards Căpâlna, 2.5 miles down the valley, but we set off upwards to the fortress of Costeşti-Blidaru.

A group of children in traditional Romanian dress passed us on their way to the fair. They saw me fumbling to grab my camera for a hasty photo, but were having none of that. They beamed as they stopped and formed up to pose for me. They looked beautiful in their pristine and brightly coloured costumes. I thanked them profusely. Yet another warm, spontaneous gesture of kindness from the people of Romania.

The mile up to Costeşti-Blidaru seemed especially long. It was steeply uphill and rough underfoot, although we were fine in our trusty sandals. A characterful beech forest shaded our steps and gave way to gnarly, twisted birch trees the higher we got. Tiny crystals of mica in the soil endowed the path with a magical, understated sparkle as the dappled sunlight danced through the branches. A French couple whom we passed put the scenery into words.

"Every tree is beautiful!"

They were hiking up the full length of the valley, planning to wild camp at the main Dacian site of Sarmizegetusa Regia. What a wonderful thing to do! Watching the sun rise over the ancient Dacian military, religious and political capital must rival witnessing the summer solstice at Stonehenge.

A sudden, shrill screech shattered the silence. Ruby shot towards us like a bullet. A large, winged insect shared the frame, so we surmised that she might have been stung. Ever the brave princess, she continued to scream like a banshee as we checked her over. Her yelps and howls emphasised her point that she had completely lost the use of her legs and needed to be cuddled and carried for the rest of the day, if not for life.

In a grassy clearing, near the top of the climb, we met a Romanian lady and her son. Petrified by the other-worldly wails that had echoed around the peaceful forest, they had feared it was a wolf or bear attack. They were visibly relieved when we explained, but were extremely concerned about Ruby.

"Her leg is broken!" the lady pronounced.

Not an unreasonable conclusion. Ruby's shrieks certainly suggested a level of pain in keeping with a multiple amputation without anaesthetic, carried out by a drunkard in a blindfold with a butter-knife.

We said that her leg was fine, although to be fair to Ruby, a swelling of respectable dimensions was beginning to rise on her rump.

"Is this the fortress?" we were looking at a rough pile of sticks that had once been a gate.

"My country needs to do more!" the lady declared as she indicated the remains of the grand entrance to the UNESCO World Heritage Site. We suggested that Romania had other priorities, and the lady rightly said:

"But it is beautiful!"

Developing tourism would certainly help the country along its road to success.

I mentioned earlier that Romania is not big on signage. At the gate, a plaque no more than four inches square, tucked in the bushes, proclaimed the site's UNESCO status.

Through the portal, we were greeted by a rank of three pear-shaped hay ricks in a buzzing wildflower meadow. Propped up by a tripod of wooden legs, they stood about eight feet tall and levelled their challenge directly to the front of the fortress. They put me in mind of the windmills with whom Don Quixote did battle, mistaking them for giants.

White limestone blocks outlined the shape of the ruined walls. Although barely visible through the lush grass, a few rusting signs did explain the significance of each area. At 2,316ft, the site had a commanding 360-degree view of the surrounding mountains. We had the fortress entirely to ourselves. It was incredibly moving to savour the views, the atmosphere and the history in absolute peace and solitude. It is how I yearn to enjoy sites such as Machu Picchu or Angkor Wat. Maybe Costești-Blidaru should attract more visitors, but this was a real privilege. Sometimes, treading your own path rather than following the masses does yield very rich rewards.

The demise of the Dacian civilisation and the downfall of Costești-Blidaru had started with the Roman conquest of 102AD. After this, the fortress was rebuilt by the Dacian King, Decebal, during a short and uneasy truce with Rome. However, in 106AD, it was destroyed utterly by Emperor Trajan. Trajan's column in Rome was built to celebrate his conquest of Dacia.

As we made our descent, Rosie and Lani decided to copy the Romans and invaded a Romanian couple's picnic. Embarrassed, I called them back.

"Don't worry. We adore dogs. We have seven of our own!"

"Wow," I replied. "Someone who has more dogs than us!"

They smiled. "There are just so many dogs in need in Romania."

It was oddly prophetic. Soon, we would discover how easy it is to collect dogs in Romania.

Back in Costești, the Fab Four made another cooling foray into the river. We didn't find Kai's lost lead. Like the path, the earth on the riverbanks contained mica, which captured sunbeams and swirled like a golden snowstorm in the water as we paddled. A string closure from Mark's 'Mutt's Nuts' backpack made a jury-rigged lead for Kai as we went to investigate the fair, which occupied large fields on either side of the road. Our wanderings revealed mainly stalls selling food or colourful tat.

There was no shade and we decided that any further Dacian ruins might be beyond our injured princess. Brave Ruby had not regained the use of her legs for the entire descent from the fortress and had to be carried around the fair. In between, she did summon the strength to enter her favourite element, however, trotting happily around in the river with her tail rotating like a helicopter blade. I think I heard her mumble something about healing waters.

...

Everybody knows that vampires come from Transylvania, but did you know about the werewolves? The legends of men turning into wolves originated with the Dacian wolf-cult. Dacians growled and howled as they went into battle, wearing wolf-skins and masks. In the myth of The Great White Wolf, Dacian Top God, Zalmoxis, transforms a man into a werewolf. Even the word 'Dacian' comes from 'daos', which means 'wolves'. Like the Direwolves in Game of Thrones, Dacian werewolves were not monsters or enemies, but protectors.

We stopped in the town of Orăştie to photograph the magnificent bronze sculpture of the Dacian Draco, the snarling, wolf-headed standard that the Dacians carried into battle. With a fabric tube to the rear of a metal head, the Draco was thought to have started life as a device to measure the wind strength and direction to help archers to aim their arrows. However, air passing through the tube made it swirl and writhe as though it were alive and when galloped into battle, the hollow, metal head emitted a howl that terrified everyone who heard it. Rather like our little Ruby.

Tourists might photograph the sculpture because the wolf is such an important symbol in Dacian and Romanian culture, because the Draco inspired bravery and courage, or simply because it is a thing of beauty. We photographed it for all of these reasons, but mostly because Mark had decided that it would form the basis of his next tattoo.

...

Back at the campsite, our Romanian neighbour, Miron, popped around again. He lived in Bucharest but had brought his family to see his home town. He gave us a small, plastic water bottle filled with pálinka; a plum brandy, which is Romania's national drink. This particular example had been lovingly fermented and home-distilled to the point of being almost vaporous by Miron's uncle.

"Be careful with it," he urged. "It's about fifty per cent alcohol."

We thanked him profusely for his kindness, but checked, "Are you sure you don't want it yourself?"

"My Uncle gives us at least two litres every time we visit."

We sensed that Miron's liver, along with the livers of his close family and friends, was silently beseeching us to accept.

Since I have conducted in-depth research, now seems a good time to guide you through the labyrinth of Romanian plum-liquor terminology as I understand it. So here goes: pálinka and țuică are both made from plums, but pálinka is generally more alcoholic, since it is twice- or thrice- distilled. Or it might just be that pálinka is a word of Hungarian origin for țuică, or refers to țuică made in the Ardeal region. Or it might just all be the same thing.

According to tradition, distillation must take place in a brass still over wood or charcoal. However, since gas is more controllable, it gives more consistent results. The heat source probably makes little difference to the final product, but don't mention gas to pálinka purists – or Romanian Standards.

Horíncă, jinars or fățată are all terms for "very strong țuică" – or might simply be different names for țuică in different regions. None of these should be confused with slivovitz. Slivovitz is still plums, but ground plum stones are added to the fermentation to give a nutty flavour. Popular in other Balkan countries, slivovitz is less common in Romania.

Although țuică can be drunk straight from the still, old țuică (țuică bătrână) is aged in oak barrels, while "țuică cu fruct" is țuică with a whole plum inside the bottle (a plum centre!).

"How do they do that?" I hear you ask in wonder.

Here, I shall share with you a special Romanian secret. Just place an empty bottle over the branch of a plum tree in Spring and then Hey...

...wait three months...

...Presto!

A whole fruit has grown inside the bottle. (Note – this is not the method used for model ships.)

Rachiu is the same drink but made with other fruit. Although rachiu can also be made with plums.

Phew. I'm glad that we've got that cleared up. I hope that you have been keeping up as there will be a test later. And I am hoping that during my careful fact-checking, Lia wasn't just spinning me a plum line.

Lia informed us that our pálinka was a bit 'light-weight'. Her grandparents considered 70 per cent alcohol more acceptable. For context, a bottle of vodka is usually around 40 per cent.

Romania is one of Europe's top plum-producers. I could make another pun around 'plum centre' here, but I won't, because that would be plumbing the depths.

Lia also wowed me with the numerous different types of Romanian plum jam, although statistics suggest that over 75 per cent of Romanian plums end up as alcohol. Even though it is traditionally served in a small glass to be sipped before a meal, pálinka represents 40 per cent of Romania's alcoholic beverage consumption. And it is used on special occasions instead of wine to propose a toast.

"*Noroc* – Cheers!"

With a sense of wonder, we opened the lid to savour the soft bouquet of our pálinka. It nearly knocked us out.

We wetted our lips (tasted it) and then put it in the fridge. We were reasonably hopeful that, given time, it might just evaporate.

In the meantime, we suspected that the fumes might help to clean and sterilise the fridge.

17

SARMIZEGETUSA REGIA

Romania's El Dorado

It is difficult to write about Sarmizegetusa Regia.

Romania's unashamed beauty already threatened to exhaust my repertoire of superlatives. Then all of a sudden, something like Sarmizegetusa comes along, whacks you in the solar plexus and leaves you speechless.

From Costeşti, it was a beautiful, forested drive up to the remote car park. From there, we hiked the last mile along a cobbled road, which inclined gently, bordered by dense forest. At the entrance, the Pawsome Foursome were allowed in without their leads, since there were stray dogs on the site. However, Mark received a respectful request to put on his shirt.

Hidden in a silent clearing in a beech forest, atop a plateau nearly 4,000ft high, lies a 2000-year old relic, a 7.5-acre quadrangle, with five terraces, hewn out of the mountainside by hand. The area is contained within *murus Dacius* – Dacian walls, built from large limestone blocks. They sit together without mortar, yet were strong and flexible enough to withstand Roman siege engines.

Back in the iron age, on this remote hilltop, the blue-eyed, blond- or red-haired Dacians enjoyed an unbelievably sophisticated lifestyle. Roads paved with mica schist criss-crossed the hill and a system of ceramic pipes brought drinking water into the homes of the nobility. It was the Dacian capital and sacred centre and it was very, very rich.

Sarmizegetusa Regia is, perhaps, Romania's 'El Dorado' – City of Gold. After sacking the Dacian holy city, Trajan allegedly carted off 250 tonnes of gold and 500 tonnes of silver, one of the largest hauls of treasure in the ancient world. The area retained its reputation for hidden riches for two millennia. As if to prove the staggering wealth of the Dacian civilisation, even after 2000 years of pilfering, there was still gold in them there hills.

As communism ended and the first metal detectors became available in Romania, the site was looted. It was Romania's Gold Rush. Thousands of gold coins were found along with more than twenty solid-gold spiral bracelets, some of which weighed up to a kilogramme each. As these appeared at sales and auctions around the world, some were recovered and can be seen in the National History Museum in Bucharest, although many are still missing. There are anecdotal reports of locals finding huge stashes of gold in relatives' chimneys.

None of the recovered Dacian coins and jewellery showed any signs of wear. It is thought that, far from being currency or jewellery, gold objects were produced primarily as offerings to the gods.

...

The remains of Sarmizegetusa's temples were unbelievably atmospheric. Although it was the height of the August holiday season, there were fewer than a dozen visitors within the site.

We passed through the massive stone walls of the fortification, which would originally have been 10ft thick and 15ft high. A 700ft, limestone-paved processionary road led from the fortress into the sacred zone. It is believed that the road was originally shaded by a roof of wooden shingle tiles, supported by poles placed on limestone plinths. As the temple precinct opened out before us, we were greeted by one of those ferocious Romanian stray dogs. A long-haired, white-and-black Collie bowled straight up to us and immediately rolled over to demand a tummy tickle.

The sacred area is laid out on two terraces, supported by limestone walls. Here, we found the remains of seven structures; two circular sanctuaries and five rectangular temples, built from limestone and andesite (a volcanic rock). Although it was destroyed convincingly by the Romans, the bases of the temple columns and pillars are still clearly visible in regular patterns.

The large, circular sanctuary has been reconstructed. A D-shaped centre of wooden poles is surrounded by concentric timber circles and a low, andesite-stone kerb. It reminded me of a wooden Stonehenge – and remarkably, the layouts of the two monuments have striking similarities. The sanctuary is believed to be an ingenious Dacian calendar, accurate to one day in 8,840 years.

With a 25ft diameter, the Andesite Sun disc has ten narrow channels or 'rays' emanating from its centre. A stone extension, like a compass needle, protrudes from the circle and points north. A drainage channel connected to the 'rays' has led to speculation that the Andesite Sun was used as an altar for blood sacrifices. It is also widely believed that it could be Romania's first sundial; the mathematics associated with its design show that it could have been used to predict the solstices and equinoxes. Of course, it may have been used for both functions.

A huge number of artefacts were recovered from the houses, workshops and granaries on the lower terraces, including a medical kit comprising of a scalpel, tweezers, powdered pumice and medicine vials.

As with Stonehenge, ley lines and mysterious energies reputedly converge at Sarmizegetusa. I am not big on mysticism, but the quiet, spiritual ambience of the place was extraordinary. It reminded me of the blurry, weather interface in Otočec, although here, the blurring was between present and past. It seemed possible to reach through the curtain of time and draw yourself closer to a bygone age; to walk more intimately in the footsteps of an ancient people. I found it incredibly moving. Sarmizegetusa left me with a remarkable sense of history and myth; it is definitely one not to be missed.

However, as our lady at Costești-Blidaru said, Romania could do more. Information was not readily available anywhere. There is a second reason why I found Sarmizegetusa difficult to write about. This short piece took hours research – I even had to resort to academic papers.

...

The stray Collie followed us back to the car park. I heard the sliding door of the van open.

"We can't take him home!"

"I'm just getting some food for him…" Mark may have fibbed.

The Collie soon polished off a full tin of the beef and salmon that our pampered pooches had begun to refuse. We lectured them on how lucky they were.

Now, just Mark and I were starving. A restaurant which promised Dacian specialities tempted us. I was so looking forward to my first bulz, a traditional dish made from polenta (corn meal) served with melted cheese.

I asked if dogs were allowed, the waitress said not. On our way back down to the car park, another waitress stopped us.

"You're not staying?"

"We can't come in with the dogs."

"Of course you can!"

She showed us around to an outside terrace. I collected menus and she assured us that she would come back in five minutes. We waited fifteen minutes and then conducted a thorough search of the premises. There was no-one to be seen, so we left.

At the little café in Conteşta, we felt better for an unremarkable pork burger. A Belgian couple joined us on the next table; we invited ourselves over to gawp at his dessert.

"What's that?" we drooled.

"Papanaşi," he replied.

We ordered one immediately.

If Stefan's recommendation on the Transalpina was going to be better than this one, we couldn't wait. Papanaşi – it was love at first bite.

18

ENLIGHTENMENT IN ALBA IULIA

The Double-Star Fortress: Romania's Best-Kept Secret?

Come with me to an iconic citadel, with three fortresses and a history which spans two millennia. It is irrevocably bound to citizens' rights and was fundamental to the birth of modern Romania. Important enough to be referred to as Romania's 'other capital', it's not yet made the World Heritage list, so for the moment, I promise that we will have it to ourselves.

Alba Iulia started life as the Roman capital of the conquered province of Dacia in 106AD. You can still see the remains of the gate, walls and roads of the Roman castrum (fort). Known as Apulum, it housed Julius Caesar's elite XIII "Gemina" Legion for nearly two centuries.

Scroll forward to the 16th and 17th centuries; the Roman fortification was expanded and incorporated into the medieval capital of the kingdom of Romanians. Its Slavic name 'Bălgrad' means 'White Castle'.

In the 18th century, along came the Austro-Hungarian Habsburgs, who engineered the magnificent third incarnation of the fortress. They named it Alba Carolina (Karlsburg) in honour of the emperor Carol VI. Alba Carolina is the largest citadel in Romania, constructed in the shape of wobbly, seven-pointed star – one of the most advanced defensive systems of the time.

Only 100 years ago, Alba Iulia was the capital of Transylvania, an independent state. At the end of WWI, following the collapse of the Austro-Hungarian Empire, elected representatives voted unanimously to unite Transylvania with Romania. Unification was declared in Alba Iulia on 1st December 1918, a date now celebrated annually as Romania's National Day. The coronation of the united Romania's first monarchs, King Ferdinand I and Queen Marie, took place in Alba Iulia, sealing its reputation as 'The Other Capital' or 'The Capital of the Union'.

Our first view, apart from the pervasive communist concrete on the outskirts, was the opulent Orthodox Catedrala Încoronări, the Coronation Cathedral, and Sfântul Mihail, the Roman Catholic Cathedral of St Michael, which dates back to the 1200s. Both shimmered in brilliant sunshine atop the imposing brick walls of the citadel.

Strolling down Strada Mihai Viteazul, we encountered a few of the twenty-five life-sized bronze statues of 17th-century townsfolk. We met the soldier, the florist with her basket of roses, a peasant woman resting on a bench and even a group of children playing with a puppy.

This brought us to the Third Gate, the largest of the seven gates and the citadel's main entrance, which is also the symbol of Alba Iulia. At least 100ft high, it is an immense, white, triumphal arch, decorated with ornate Baroque reliefs on both faces and topped by a Habsburg, Emperor Carol VI, on his horse.

I mentioned Alba Iulia's significance in the struggle for citizens' rights. The Third Gate contains the small cell where Horea, the leader of the peasant riot in 1784, was held before his execution. Just beyond the gate is a 75ft obelisk, built in 1937 to honour Horea, Cloşca and Crişan, the martyred leaders of the uprising. Crişan hanged himself the night before the execution. Perhaps he knew what was coming. Horea and Cloşca met their end tied to a huge 'Catherine wheel', which was rolled up and down the hill until they were crushed to death. This brutal torture is named after the virgin martyr Saint Catherine of Alexandria, whose spiked breaking wheel shattered at her touch. It was not a happy ending, though, since pagan emperor Maxentius then had her beheaded.

The legacy of the peasant martyrs was the 1785 'Patent for the Abolition of Serfdom for Transylvania'. Enacted by Habsburg Emperor Joseph II, it heralded a seismic change which resonated throughout the Empire and beyond. The Patent released serfs from the absolute control of their landlords. Serfs were spared beatings, given the right to choose marriage partners, could move between estates and obtain justice from the crown, rather than their lords' own courts.

The Patent also limited the landlords' demand for unpaid labour to three days per week and capped the price for a serf to buy their freedom. It all sounds very progressive, although when you discover that Emperor Jo was Marie Antoinette's brother, you might not be surprised to find that his motivations were not entirely altruistic.

Traditionally, nobles and churchmen were exempt from paying taxes. In an economy based on agriculture, granting serfs freedom from economic subjugation by their lords also granted them their greatest freedom; the freedom to pay taxes to fund their emperor.

...

With pups in tow, we had to admire the many historic buildings in the citadel from the outside, although we could all walk leads-off around the Vauban fortifications.

Marquis de Vauban was a 17th-century French military engineer. His skills lay in fortress design and construction, although he was also a brilliant tactician, who focussed on capturing defensive fortifications with minimal bloodshed. Vauban's designs and strategies were so successful that they persisted for nearly three hundred years. You will see Vauban fortifications all over Europe; not least the UNESCO-listed 'Twelve Fortifications of Vauban' dotted along the French border.

The invention of powerful new weapons had made medieval castles vulnerable. Cannon fire could easily destroy perpendicular masonry walls. At the same time, regular shapes often denied the defenders a good angle of fire, which granted the enemy cover to undermine walls in relative safety.

Vauban's polygonal fortifications cleverly overcame all of these disadvantages. Multiple, low but wide, brick walls were filled with earth and separated by dry ditches. Brick absorbs the destructive power of cannon, since it does not shatter like stone, while the star-shape afforded defenders many different angles of fire. Vauban's Alba Carolina has three, concentric, star-shaped brick walls, separated by deep ditches.

It was a pleasant stroll around the perimeter, popular with horse-drawn tours and bicycles. After a coffee at one of the many of street cafés, we called it a day about half-way around the 7.5-mile circuit. We'd had our fun. Now, there was the real business of the day to be addressed: the purchase of a data SIM card on Stefan's recommendation.

We homed in on the tourist office, whose manager was enthusiastic and helpful. She plied us with bags full of information and even presented us with a beautiful, full-colour hardback about the Merry Cemetery in Maramureş, way up north.

A young, Indian medical student, who spoke twelve languages, was volunteering in the office. Later, as we were searching for the Vodafone shop, we ran into him again. He was on his way home, but rather than giving us directions, he walked us to the shop door and there, we scored a SIM card with 150GB of data for €15 per month.

As for the city's remaining gates, the gardens and the changing of the guard that we had missed at 12pm? Well, we would just have to come back.

19

AUREL VLAICU TO CAMPING ANANAS, CISNĂDIOARA, NEAR SIBIU

"I like your parrot!"; The Inequalities of a Global Economy
& The King of Wines

Unlike childbirth, it came out a lot easier than it went in.

By that, I mean the caravan. I had enlisted the help of Dennis and was positioned strategically with my camera to capture the reverse of the 'honeymoon fit'. However, the exit produced no drama, spectacle or theatrics.

It was a short-ish, pleasant drive to Sibiu, one of the seven citadels founded by the Transylvanian Saxons. In a minor gesture of malice, Naffsat directed us, caravan and all, the wrong way around Sibiu's one-way system. Luckily, I rumbled its pitiless quest for vengeance and assumed command. A hasty scan of the map determined that we needed to follow signs to Păltiniş, then turn off when we were half way there.

Of course, Mark and I were gossiping away and completely missed the junction. The narrow road left us no option but to drive all the way to Păltiniş. As we admired the first and highest mountain resort in Romania, a crowd gathered to admire our U-turn, which took place amid an installation of abandoned trams, stranded to rust artfully around the town centre.

Reception was closed until 4pm, so we pulled into a quiet corner of Camp Ananas and got the kettle on. Kismet overlooked a vampire castle on the hill opposite. Later, we discovered that it was a fortified church, not a castle, but it looked very Transylvanian, with a full moon hanging above, in a pinky-mauve, afternoon sky.

"I like your parrot!" I greeted Long John Silver; a slim, dark-haired and deeply-tanned young man who walked past with a green parakeet on his shoulder.

"Where are you from?" he enquired.

"England."

"Unlucky you!" replied a cut-glass accent.

This was Jake, a fellow Brit. After an animated, half-hour chat, my offer of a cup of PG Tips sealed the deal. We were firm friends.

Jake and his Canadian wife Kate had been in Romania for two years and were Living their Dream by touring the world. Jake explained that Kate was a wonderful lady, but had no comprehension of his need for PG tips. And Marmite. With the unbridled excitement of a child on Christmas Eve, Jake revealed that a

Scottish chap in the village had promised to supply him with a jar the following day.

Kate and Jake had just traded in their 6x6-wheel truck and were temporarily ensconced in a higgledy-piggledy homestead composed of a small campervan and several large tents. They were awaiting delivery of an 8x8 converted army truck, in which they intended to tour Africa. Kate was a digital nomad while Jake, only in his late twenties, was retired. Before you get jealous, though, let me share with you the shocking events that led to Jake's early retirement. Jake suffered constant pain due to life-changing injuries sustained in the defence of the realm. On active service, he had been shot in the chest by Somali Pirates and left for dead.

I wouldn't wish anyone Jake's journey but, as with us, the outcome ultimately had many positives. Retired in his mid-twenties, able to travel and loving it, Jake was sensible enough to look at the benefits rather than being embittered by the terrible situation that had led him there.

We dined with Kate and Jake. In what other sphere of life can you meet someone for a few minutes and be invited to dinner for a warm and entertaining evening? They introduced the rest of the family: dogs Jonti, a stray from Bucharest and Stella, a Cretan Hunter, recovered from a motorway in Crete. Coco the parrot was another Romanian refugee. Mark admired the new leather corner suite that they had bought that day, but was curious to know:

"How are you going to transport that?"

"It deflates!" Jake exclaimed. "I bought it in Carrefours. You can buy anything in Carrefours."

An inflatable sofa – and it was surprisingly comfortable.

Kate and Jake filled us in on the recent history of our pitch. It had been occupied for a few months by Frank. However, Frank had departed suddenly, following a dinner date with Kate and Jake.

"We arrived nine minutes late and he told us that dinner was 'gone.'" Kate said. Strangely, the following day, Frank was also 'gone'.

...

"Jackie! Jackie!" Jake called for me at the caravan door the following morning. "I've been to the farmers' market. I've brought you fresh bread from a lady who bakes it herself and some local sheep cheese. Have some strawberries too. We can't eat them all and they won't keep."

Jake grinned and performed the big reveal. In both hands, cradled with gentle reverence as though it were a priceless Fabergé egg, he showed us his jar of Marmite.

The 'vampirey' church of St Michael on the hill above Cisnădioara beckoned that day. It was a pleasantly shaded, off-lead walk up Mihail Hill, from which the village got its German name Michelsberg, or Michael's Hill. The 12th-century church is one of the oldest monuments around Sibiu, built in the Romanesque style, which is rare in the area.

There are over 150 fortified churches in Transylvania, of which seven are World Heritage Sites. They were constructed to protect villagers from frequent Ottoman attacks. St Michael's had both atmosphere and sensational views over Sibiu and back to the campsite. And lacking UNESCO status, we had it to ourselves.

Originally, the now ruined defensive walls would have been around 20ft high. Gaps allowed defenders to push large rocks downhill at attackers. Before getting married, it was the duty of every man in the village to roll a boulder uphill to the church, to maintain the supply of ammunition. A few such stones are still visible, lying around the churchyard.

We spent the evening with Constantin and Diana, a couple whom we had first met over a bottle of wine at Aurel Vlaicu.

Constantin worked for an international telecoms company and spent half of his time in the UK, although he was paid the going rate for Romania. His UK colleagues, doing the same job, were paid three or four times more. I was outraged on his behalf. Constantin was sanguine and accepting.

"I am paid well and I like the lifestyle in Romania."

In his eyes, he had the best deal. In a global economy, there are winners and losers, but I suppose that the lines are blurred as to who are the lucky ones.

At Aurel Vlaicu, we had discussed Romanian wines

with Constantin. We had arranged to meet again at Camping Ananas, so he had kindly brought a few of his favourites for us to try, as well as a special bottle from Georgia. Constantin told us about Red Miniş, christened 'The King of Wines' 150 years ago in London. We couldn't believe that we had spent time in Miniş and missed it!

20

A STROLL AROUND SIBIU

European City of Culture 2007 & Occasional Capital of Transylvania

'Gilberts' is my name for those annoying rafts of tannin and carbonates that you get on a cup of tea made with hard water. I can cope with the many hardships of travel, but draw the line at Gilberts on me cuppa.

The relatively small size of our caravan fridge had forced us to purchase a non-standard water-filter jug. However, our supply of non-standard water filters seemed to have disappeared into the caravan's Bermuda Triangle. I had no idea how difficult it would be to replace anything as bourgeois as a water filter in Romania. Even market-leader Brita was unavailable online, and their nearest supplier was in Bucharest. I declared a Gilbert emergency, although even that didn't outrank the terror of a trip to big, bad Bucharest.

The plan for the day had been to run Jake and Jonti to the vet in Cisnădie, until Jake told us about a worrying call from the vet that morning.

"The vet said he's not available because he's covering for his friend, who is a doctor at the hospital."

Unanimously, we hoped that this was either a misunderstanding due to language, or involved just bandaging rather than a full-blown foray into gynaecology and brain surgery.

Plan B was Sibiu. Parking was not easy; car parks were not marked on our map and signs confirmed Jake's warning that incorrectly parked vehicles would be towed. Jake explained the procedure,

"They leave a note where you parked to say that your vehicle has been impounded. You can ring the number on the note to get your car back, unless you can't find the note because someone else has parked on top of it. They don't have a car pound, though – and they do the paperwork afterwards – so, if you search the nearby streets, you will probably find your car and you can just drive away. Although..."

We decided that it would just be much simpler to park legally.

Sibiu was thoroughly enjoyable. In the enormous square, Piata Mare, we stopped for a coffee, overlooking the 13th-century Council Tower and The Bank of Transylvania. The puppies wanted to make a withdrawal; we told them that they couldn't go in and demand four pints.

Founded in the 1100s, Sibiu became one of largest

and richest of the seven walled Saxon citadels. The town beefed up its fortifications in the 1200s, following an attack by the Mongol grandsons of Genghis Khan, who left only 100 alive. Thirty-nine defensive towers, five bulwarks, four gates and five artillery batteries made Sibiu one of the most powerful strongholds in Europe.

Sibiu has an upper town and lower town. In the upper town, Brukenthal Palace now houses the Brukenthal National Museum. It is the oldest museum in Romania and among the oldest in Europe, pre-dating the Louvre by three years.

We descended to the lower town near the 'Bridge of Lies'. Legend has it that the bridge will creak when someone standing on it is creative with the truth. In the Middle Ages, dishonest merchants and naughty girls would be thrown off the bridge. Today, it is the perfect spot for a selfie – and 100 per cent honesty. Just in case.

A brief rain shower led us to seek refuge in a bookshop, where we tried to buy maps. During our travels we have discovered that it is a truth universally acknowledged that buying detailed hiking maps is not easy. In Italy, we resorted to online ordering from Stanfords of London. Maps in Sibiu was a fail, but we scored a remarkable success on the water-filter front. We swung by the out-of-town shopping centre on our way home, our hopes high, considering our neighbours' inflatable sofa triumph and assertion that "You can buy anything in Carrefours." With joy akin to

Jake's Marmite delight, we returned exultant with a Brita water-filter and six spare cartridges. The sacrifice was a shelf from the fridge to fit it in, but it was worth it.

For the rest of the trip, we would be Gilbert-free.

21

A STREET DOG NAMED BLADE

How To Adopt a Romanian Stray

We had been in Romania for only two weeks but seemed destined to go the whole Romanian hog. The famous Transalpina and Transfăgărăşan highways were already on the list; we were working our way through the UNESCO World Heritage sites; then, we adopted a Romanian orphan...

There were a number of strays on the campsite, including a smallish black dog with a white chest, four smart, white socks and one floppy ear. Standing about two feet high at the shoulder, he was a similar size to our Rosie. He looked like a small Border Collie with the wiry coat of a rough Patterdale Terrier. Being smaller than the other strays, he got only leftovers; when we gave him a chew, we saw the site dog, Findus, steal it from him. To make sure that he got at least a few decent meals during our stay, we fed him if he was around.

A happy, playful chap who loved a cuddle, we looked forward to his visits. He was already popular around the site. Adopting him had obviously crossed Jake and Kate's minds, but Jonti and Stella had both suffered mistreatment and were needy. They lit up at the thought that we might take him and promised to help us to get his passport.

Some soul-searching went on inside Caravan Kismet. Reading the pet transport regulations, five seemed to be the magic number, so we would fall just the right side of the guidelines. With more than five pets, much stricter commercial rules for importing animals would apply. Travelling full-time with five dogs would not be easy. Four small Cavapoos were one thing, but the little black dog was a 'proper' dog, with presence disproportionate to his size. He was also strong and boisterous; the Fab Four liked him, but were a little scared of him. A workable solution would be to re-home him once we got back to England. I posted on Facebook that we would rescue him if we could find him a home. Within an hour, we had three offers of a forever home and this:

"I'm serious about the jabs. Email me your bank details."

I thought it was a scam. Then I read:

"Here's the deal. I will pay for the jabs if you bring him home."

It was from Nicola, a wonderful lady who follows

my blog. If you enjoy my books, thank Nicola – she persuaded me to publish these stories. We have never met, but I was humbled and overwhelmed by her kindness.

The little dog already had a lot of people on his side

...

There was no going back when, after breakfast, he popped himself to sleep underneath the caravan. Really, he had adopted us.

We asked Uva, the campsite owner, whether taking him was the right thing to do.

"Definitely. Yes! He probably won't survive the winter. The bigger dogs get work and are fed by the shepherds, but he is too small. The campsite closes in mid-October. The water freezes and there won't be much food."

With the temperature in the 30°s, it was hard to comprehend the sign for snow chains just outside the campsite. Knowing that it would be a death sentence, we couldn't leave him. The Fab Four was about to become the Famous Five.

We needed a name.

"He's a cheerful little boy. What's the Romanian for 'happy'?"

"'Fericit' – it sounds like 'Very Shit', so maybe not..."

We tried on 'Chizzie' – from his home town, Cisnădioara – but he didn't look like a Chizzie. Or a 'Vlad', since we were in Transylvania.

Then, we thought about one of our favourite films, *Blade – The Vampire Slayer*. It suited him perfectly.

...

The vet had finished his stint as Medical Director of the Hospital, so Mark captured Blade to take him along with Jake and Jonti. Rosie loaned Blade a lead and collar. He looked a little perplexed, but hopped willingly into Big Blue.

We guessed that Blade was about six months old. He had pearly-white teeth and was still puppy-playful. His tail seemed to be partially docked, which is common in Romania. Uva explained.

"Supposedly, it makes dogs more aggressive. The tail is important in communication, so perhaps it just causes misunderstandings, which look like aggression."

We wondered whether that meant that he might once have been owned, although months later we met Blade's double in the UK and he had a naturally short tail, exactly like Blade's, so we will never know.

The vet advised a bath followed by a flea and worm treatment. Later, I saw Mark chasing a soapy dog around the campsite. In other circumstances, it would have been funny.

"I'm afraid that I've lost his trust. He was fine when I wetted him and lathered him up, but he went into a blind panic and slipped his collar when I started to rinse him."

Blade was coaxed back with some food, then we cuddled and reassured him as we rinsed him off as best we could with cups of water. Nevertheless, our first night together in the caravan was with a slightly shampooey stray. We didn't want to tether him outdoors in case another dog came along or he got tangled. Jake and Kate offered to put him up for the night in their outer tent, but since we were going to have to cohabit successfully for the next few months, we thought it best to start as we meant to go on.

To prepare him for a home that might prefer to keep dogs off the furniture, we made Blade a comfy nest between the sofas at the front of the caravan. In addition, to give The Pawsome Foursome respite from his boisterous play, our bed was designated a Blade-Free Zone.

Inside the caravan, Blade stuck to the rules. We had a clean, dry night and he woke us up at 6:40am to go out for a poo.

...

Eat, Play, Love – A Letter from Blade

I've won over some new humans. I came to visit the four Frou Frou dogs and gave their Dogfather a cuddle. He started feeding me, so the training is working brilliantly. Then he said that I could go with them to England, so I should write letters for my new mum and dad.

They put a lead on me and we went for a walk to the church. They're new here, so they probably didn't want to get lost, although they said, "You wouldn't get that at Legoland!" when the lady let them in for free because they had visited the other day. If that's true, I can't believe they've forgotten the way already! Their sense of direction must be terrible.

Anyway, I got them there safely and they let me off the lead in the churchyard. They said it was an 'experiment'. I guess they wanted to see if they could get back without me.

When I ran over to the only gate in the walls, the Dogfather blocked it. He put me back on the lead. He must have forgotten the way at the last minute and needed me to show him. I don't mind keeping an eye on them and I can certainly help with all that spare food. The Frou Frous told me they've got the EU Food Mountain in their van and I can eat up all the beef and salmon.

22

DRIVING THE TRANSALPINA

The Highest Road in Romania

The Transalpina mountain pass was on our list, not least to sample Stefan's Premier Papanași.

Kate and Jake agreed to look after Blade; we felt that five hours of winding roads would not be the best introduction to motor travel. Jake planned to go to the Carrefours, so we left him with a shopping list of essentials for Blade.

The Transalpina (DN67C) crosses the Parâng range of the Southern Carpathians and runs ninety-two miles north to south, linking Sebeş with Novaci. It is the highest road in Romania, reaching 7,037ft at Pasul Urdele, but is less well-known than the Trans-făgărăşan. That is very much part of its charm. It is generally less busy and the pristine, natural scenery has remained largely undisturbed as the road was only paved and opened to the public in 2015.

Although it is a very strategic road, its origins are unclear. Some say that it was built by the Romans during their campaign against Dacia. It gets a mention in 18th-century documents and was used as a mountain crossing by shepherds. It was rebuilt by the Germans during WWI, but fell into disrepair due to a lack of funds. In the 1930s, King Carol II started to pave the road, which is why it is sometimes called 'The King's Road – Drumul Regelui', although its vertiginous drops have led others to christen it 'The Devil's Path'.

The plan had been to call in at the UNESCO fortified church at Calnic, but we decided to leave it when we failed to reach the Transalpina efficiently. Naffsat cunningly directed us straight through the centre of Sibiu; it would have been easier – and forty minutes shorter – to have joined the autoroute at Cisnădie.

Accidentally, we avoided the official start of the Transalpina entirely. Approaching from Sibiu, Naffsat opted for a cross-country shortcut, although I would not have missed the stunning villages that we passed through for the world. Saliste, Tilisca, Rod, Poianu, Sibiuli and Jina were dazzling and to add to the atmosphere, full of life. We passed little old ladies in black wearing their headscarves and men with hats that looked like a tall bowler with no rim. I don't know if it was a holy day or whether the gathering just happens every Wednesday, but villagers were out in force, everywhere we went.

The landscape early on reminded us of Maui –

creased and folded mountains covered in lush, green vegetation; rather like Jurassic Park. Sandy soil meant that the edges of the roads were crumbling. As we rose to the top of a plateau with extensive views, we passed a horse and cart with the foal running free beside the mare.

The lake, Lacul Oaşa, boasted a selection of stalls. I was starving, so we stopped for a bite to eat, our first lángos. A Hungarian street treat, its name comes from 'láng' meaning 'flame'. Introduced by the Turks, it is a freshly-cooked flat-bread made with yeast dough, served with a variety of toppings. We opted for sheep cheese and garlic mayonnaise. It was tangy and delicious – and guaranteed to keep the vampires at bay.

The lángos cost just over £1 each and were so enormous that Mark had to finish mine. I needed coffee, but was told that there was no electricity for the coffee machine. With typical Romanian generosity, a young stall-holder offered to boil up some water on the gas and charged me less than £1 for my coffee. As we waited for the water to boil, he told me his dream, to study the natural world in America. I gave him a large tip in the hope that it might help a little.

At Hanul Haiducilor, we stopped to sample Stefan's Ultimate Papanaşi. We settled at a picnic table in the woods and can say that it was a good papanaşi. A very good papanaşi. But it was not our favourite.

The best so far was one that cost virtually nothing in an unassuming roadside restaurant in Slimnic. Hanul Haiducilor also served bulz, but I was too full of lángos and papanași. Bulz would have to wait for another day.

Re-joining the E81 from the Transalpina was terrifying. Convoys of huge lorries thundered towards us with the slightest clearance and Romania Mania once more came to the fore. A few times, had we not braked sharply, cars overtaking us on blind bends would have ploughed head-on into 40-tonnes of death.

Blade bounced with delight when we got back. Although he had engaged with people passing throughout the day, Kate told us that he hadn't greeted anyone so enthusiastically. He had spent the whole day tethered – and content. We had worried that he might fight against being confined. By some estimates, dogs have been domesticated for 40,000 years. As Uva said:

"Perhaps he's just happy to know that he belongs to someone."

Kate and Jake refused to take any money for his new lead, collar, tag and bowl. It was their present to him as he started his new life.

23

MOVE TO CAMP AQUARIS, SIGHIȘOARA

Help is Hindrance

As we had our final morning brew with Jake, I presented him with a bag of precious, irreplaceable PG Tips teabags. In no doubt as to the magnitude of such a gift, he thanked me with the awed appreciation of a transplant patient to whom I had offered one of my kidneys.

Sorting out Blade had cost us some time. Our plan had been to stop at Mediaș, a historic, fortified city, but we pushed straight on to Sighișoara. This saved one moving day, but I was determined that the distraction of Sighișoara, one of the oldest and best-preserved fortified citadels in Europe, wouldn't mean that I missed out on the Mediaș Museum of Natural Gas.

Blade had asked to go out again at exactly 6:40am. When we opened Big Blue's door to load up, he jumped in as if to say "Don't go without me!" – even though he had been sick in the van on the way to the vet yesterday.

Big Blue has been modified to accommodate our Travelling Cavapoos. She is wider than a car, with a middle 'mate's' seat, and Mark built a comfy, full-width dog bed behind the bulkhead. Nevertheless, five dogs inside was pretty cosy.

En route, I suddenly remembered what it was besides a car harness that I had wanted Mark to buy in preparation for our journey. Wet wipes. The reminder came from Blade as he vomited copiously. We contained the worst of it with our never-ending supply of dog blankets. However, aside from blowing chunks, he seemed to cope admirably with his first long journey. He was obviously a little scared – his eyes were on stalks – but eventually he curled up next to me. We thought that he would soon get used to this travelling lark. He would need to; we had a major scare.

"Romania is an unlisted country." A friend's email suggested that crossing borders and taking Blade back to the UK might not be as straightforward as we had first thought.

Never one to overreact, I launched into a full panic.

To enter the UK from an unlisted country, a 'titer test' is required. The test, which must be carried out by an EU approved laboratory, checks antibody levels in the blood to ensure that the rabies jab was effective. Getting the test was not a problem. The drawback was the timescale – it would take at least four months. The pet can't travel for three months from the date of the blood sample, which can only be taken 30 days or more after the rabies vaccination.

All of a sudden, our travel plans had been thrown into disarray.

Frantic internet research finally pinpointed that the article was from 2003, which pre-dated Romania joining the EU in 2007.

We breathed a huge sigh of relief. Despite being a legitimate EU Citizen, we knew that Blade could still not enter the UK until 21 days after his rabies vaccination; before this, the vaccination is not deemed effective. On an extended tour, this posed no problem for us, but could be a deal-breaker for anyone thinking of adopting an animal on a shorter trip.

Even so, that horribly uncomfortable feeling of "We'll believe it when we see it..." lingered in the pit of our stomachs. Although we planned to stay in Romania until Blade's rabies vaccine was effective, we decided to route ourselves out via Schengen borders. This would avoid any need for the meeting of officialdom with pet passports. The UK Government website declared its acceptance of pet passports from all EU countries, but despite seeing it in black-and-white, our antennae of angst had started to wag. We had no idea what we would do if Blade was refused admission to any of the countries that we needed to cross in order to get home – or if he was turned back at the UK border.

...

Our next stop, Campsite Aquaris, had been recommended by Constantin and Diana. It was not the most beautiful site; it was basically a small car park with a stand of trees at one end, although it had access to a large, open-air swimming pool and was just five minutes' walk from Sighişoara. As usual, we had no booking and since the site had only eight pitches, we were glad that we had arrived mid-afternoon – and at the end of the August holiday season.

The entrance was an acutely tight, 90-degree turn from a narrow road. Further challenge was added by a van parked outside, in just the wrong place. As I checked in at reception, the van owner, along with several, swarthy mates appeared. With considerable enthusiasm, they began to wave Mark in, keeping their ever-watchful eyes on the clearance to the front. I emerged from reception just in time to see the fatal flaw in their plan; as the rear of the caravan swung round, it caught on the parked van.

I got into a frantic arm-waving-cum-shouting match with the manoeuvring committee.

"Mark. *Mark! Stop!*"

The lads beckoned and yelled louder.

"Keep coming. To me. *To me!*"

At the helm, Mark just looked confused, wondering who to obey. Thankfully, his survival instinct kicked in and he chose his wife.

Mark hopped out of Big Blue to reassess the situation and we all took five. Surveying the damage to his van, the owner grudgingly conceded that the tiny, white paint-mark on his bumper was not worth pursuing. He managed to muster an injured look, which cleverly incorporated an element of 'not my fault', then drove quite genially on his way. By now, the helping committee had vanished, like a bunch of Brexiteers asked to deliver their apocryphal £350m a week for the NHS. I gathered up several pieces of Caravan Kismet's rear from the road and noticed that the back of the caravan was hanging off. Wires swung freely in the breeze.

Caravan Confucius say – well I'm not sure. But I shall make up something about pitching by committee. Other people helping (interfering!) in a couple's well-oiled and honed routine inevitably ends in disaster.

However tempting it is to help – *don't do it!*

With the parked van gone and the helping committee dispersed, we got in with absolutely no problem.

...

"Let's leave inconspicuously, Batman. Out of the window!" is one of my favourite quotes from the old TV series. Blade arrived completely inconspicuously – straight out of Big Blue's window. Mark had unclipped his harness and, bored with all the caravan shenanigans, he had soon introduced himself to everyone on site.

"Meet Blade!" I greeted the small audience who had gathered to enjoy our committee-led rendezvous with Caravanning's Mr Cock-Up.

We cosied-up Kismet into a corner in the cool shade of a weeping willow, then Mark 'I'll have that fixed in half-an-hour' set to repairing Kismet. It was mostly just the plastic trim that had popped off and all the lights still worked, so thankfully there was no lasting damage.

The couple on the pitch next door deployed a selection of kids, aged from 0 to 13, to play with Blade. He was positively lovely with them all. It seemed strange to place so much trust in a street dog, but his business had been to charm humans on campsites. He was extremely good at it. It was the only way that he'd got fed.

Later, replete with love and attention, he hopped into Kismet and settled down. A quick learner, he just knew that this was now home. Although he had been with us for only a few days, he already responded to his name – and the command "Off".

This was in respect of the bed, the table at the front of the caravan – and humping our legs!

It was 10pm and thankfully we were all inside as Armageddon broke out.

Showers of sparks rained down on our roof from the sky as bangs, whizzes and explosions detonated all around us. We had no idea what the firework display was for, but it was directly overhead and the poor doggies were terrified.

We were so grateful that it was not Blade's first night in the caravan.

24

DOGS 'N' DRACULA: BREAKFAST IN SIGHIȘOARA

Castrum Sex & Dracula's Birthplace

It was Blade's first time away from home, so naturally, he wanted to explore. He woke us at his now customary 6:40am to remind us that a UNESCO World Heritage Site awaited. With nine guild towers, cobbled streets, Saxon houses and something to do with vampires, one of Europe's best-preserved and most beautiful fortified towns was ripe for exploration, right on our doorstep.

Since we had been up for hours, thanks to Blade, we opted to avoid the Saturday crowds and walk into Sighișoara for breakfast. From the campsite, we strolled past the striking black-and-white Orthodox Cathedral, which graced our side of the Târnava Mare River. Crossing the bridge and dual carriageway, we entered the lower town. From there, we continued through a maze of ancient alleyways, zig-zagging up cobbled stairways to Sighişoara's 'Citadel' (Cetate), atop the bluff which overlooked our campsite.

The main entrance to the town is beneath the 14th-century Clock Tower. A mahoosive 210ft high and 50 x 28ft at the base, the Clock Tower is the symbol of Sighişoara. Its roof, a mosaic of coloured tiles, topped with a bulbous spire and golden orb, was added following a fire in 1676. Also known as the Council Tower, it housed the City Council until the 1500s. The four, soaring turrets at each corner of the tower indicate that the Council had the grizzly authority to deal out the death penalty. If you are patient, you will see painted, linden-wood marionettes pop out beneath each of the two clock faces at certain times of day.

Originally known as Castrum Sex (Fort Six), the name of the town changed over the years; to Schespurch in 1298 and Civitas de Seguswar in 1397. The name Sighişoara first appeared in a written document from 1431 issued by one Vlad II, known as Vlad Dracul. This was the father of a slightly more famous Vlad Dracula, who was born that very year in Sighişoara. As a product of Romania, Vlad III even surpasses plums.

If you remember, we met Vlad Junior, known as Vlad Ţepeş (Vlad the Impaler) at Corvin. He ruled the province of Walachia from 1456 to 1462. His blood-thirsty habits – and a castle that he never even visited (Bran) – were the inspiration behind Bram Stoker's fictional creation, Count Dracula.

Of course, Blade the Vampire Slayer wanted to check out Dracula's birthplace in the Citadel Square, near the Clock Tower. The puppies had a group photo outside the unassuming end-of-terrace with what looked like yellow-ochre cob walls. Vlad Țepeș lived there with Daddy Dracul for four years until 1435, when they went for an impressive upsize to the Princely Court in Târgoviște. Then the capital of Walachia, Târgoviște is where Vlad III developed his trademark torture. He impaled the group of nobles who had brutally murdered his father and brother in their attempt to seize the throne.

And so, Vlad impaled into significance.

A wrought-iron dragon hangs above the entrance to the Vlads' pad. This was in honour of Dad Vlad, who earned the title 'Dracul' – or 'Dragon' in recognition of his bravery in wars against the Ottomans. 'Dracula', as Vlad Țepeș was known, translates as 'Son of Dracul'. Thus, in an unusual plot twist, he is named after his own movie sequel.

In medieval times, the dragon symbolised strength, wisdom, leadership and independence. However, snakey-looking dragons were also associated with the temptation of Adam and Eve. 'Dracul' translates from Romanian into English as both 'dragon' and 'devil', which seems rather apt.

We chose Casa Krauss for breakfast. Now a hotel, it had once been home to Georgius Krauss, a 17th century notary and chronicler of Transylvania's Saxon history. The gilded orb on the clock tower reputedly contains Krauss' 'The Chronical of the Clock Tower' along with other historical documents related to the city and the region's ethnic Germans. Personally, I am more inclined to believe that the orb was forged far away by a giant, who placed it there on the basis that, "who's bigger than I can take the globe, and then it's his."

Settled at a table outside, we opted for a bagel breakfast with egg and bacon. Our serene vista looked over the ancient city walls and the unevenly hexagonal Turnul Cizmarilor - the Cobblers' Tower. It was the first day of September; the light was golden and the leaves just beginning to turn. Their chestnut hues complemented the terracotta tiles on the pointed roof of the tower and gave the whole view a warm tinge of russet.

Blade sat angelically beneath the table throughout breakfast and was complimented by the waiter, who was incredulous when we told him that less than a week ago, Blade had been a stray. Later, we discovered that Blade had kept himself entertained by chewing right through his own lead and making significant progress through Rosie's. Once again, we improvised a lead for Kai from the single remaining string in Mark's Mutt's Nuts backpack. Kai is human, though, and was becoming increasingly intolerant of the indignity of being on a lead as a consequence of all this sightseeing malarkey. He dug in his heels and refused to move until we granted him freedom to trot untethered at our heels.

By 10am, we were back in the caravan. A pet shop that we passed was unable to supply a replacement lead, but despite the dearth of pet accessories, we were in full agreement that Sighișoara was a WOW and definitely one for the Bucketlist.

We loved it so much that we walked back into town that evening. Few medieval citadels are still inhabited and this gave Sighișoara a wonderful atmosphere; calm and muted, with lots of outdoor cafés, atmospheric cellar bars and even a violinist playing Vivaldi's 'Four Seasons' in the main square. Ambling through the cobbled streets, we watched the sun set over a few of the towers that we hadn't visited earlier.

Nine of the fourteen guild towers which originally graced the walls of Sighișoara survive. The guilds were medieval associations of tradespeople or craftsmen, set up to oversee business. Each guild had its own charter; a list of rules to protect its members and guarantee the quality of their work. Heavy fines were imposed for non-compliance and over time, the guilds became extremely wealthy and powerful. Sighișoara's towers are all different architecturally because each guild contributed to the defence of the citadel by building and guarding its own tower.

The surviving towers are those built by the Tanners, Tinsmiths, Ropers, Butchers, Furriers, Cobblers, Blacksmiths and the Tailors. The latter has two roads running through its base; an indication of the Tailors' wealth. I promised you nine towers; the Clock Tower completes the set.

Which brings us back to where we started.

25

TO SASCHIZ AND BEYOND – OR NOT

A Secret Castle, Cold Brew & Hadrian's Walls

Blade met Max, the baby from next door. He was beautifully gentle and affectionate with him, which I have to say was much more enthusiasm than I could muster with that full nappy...

Today's Grand Plan was the fortified churches at Saschiz, Bunești and Dârjiu, the castle at Rupea and the village of Viscri.

No 1 – the World Heritage church at Saschiz. It was closed. It was a Monday. The tourist information signboard announced that the church was closed on Mondays and Tuesdays.

But what was that up there? As we admired the wider setting, we saw a fabulous castle on a hill. No-one had mentioned the fabulous castle on the hill – and no-one knew if we could walk up to it. A scout around the village turned up a sign in Romanian that we didn't understand. It seemed to be pointing towards the castle and said '1.2km', so with pups in tow, we followed it.

On the way up, we met an English couple returning from the castle. After seeing him walk so calmly and beautifully on the lead, they were shocked and surprised to learn that Blade had been with us for only six days.

"You're doing a good job with him!"

"He makes our job very easy!"

We were beginning to notice an emerging trend with Blade; everyone he met fell in love with him.

Following a lush, green track with wild flowers bobbing in the hedgerows was like walking through a sun-kissed, rural idyll of Merrie England, but much hotter. The only other passer-by was a man driving a horse and cart. The horse's bay coat shone like a polished conker and the tassels at its temples shook as it trotted by. All Romanian horses have red tassels attached to their bridles, to ward off 'The Evil Eye'.

Later, we learned that the castle had been the villagers' refuge from frequent raids by the Mongols and Turks. It had fallen into disuse and disrepair when the fortified church was built. Needless to say, we had the ruins entirely to ourselves. In the shade of trees and cool, mossy stonework, we relaxed and explored. Then, we clambered up the walls to take in the views, which had become more sensational the higher we got. Saschiz' church tower stood out in the landscape. A slightly smaller sibling of the ornate and impressive clock tower that defines Sighişoara, it had inherited all the family's good looks.

Kai had struggled with the climb, even though it had cooled *down* to 30°C. On the descent, he resolved his temperature issues by sprawling in a muddy puddle. Everyone decided that this was a great idea and swiftly joined in.

Back in the village, we noticed a sign advertising drinks. It was near a river, so we searched for a way down to the water, to cleanse our muddy pack.

"You can reach the river from in my garden!" A tall, handsome chap with broad shoulders and a shock of black curls introduced himself. "I'm Hadrian," he said. "As in the wall."

Hadrian led us through high, wooden gates into his glorious, peaceful courtyard café, scattering kittens as he went. Hadrian helped a few stragglers over the fence and told us not to worry about the dogs.

"They'll keep their distance now that they've seen your dogs. I know the relationship between cats and dogs!"

He settled us on colourful blankets and cushions in the shade of a wooden pergola and brought bowls of water for the dogs. He offered me the use of his hose to rinse off the mud. The cobbled courtyard had the nostalgic, tumbledown charm of the farmyard set of *The Darling Buds of May*.

Hadrian was a local lad who had, until recently, worked as a chef in Leicester. In four years of hard graft in the UK, he had saved enough to buy this property in his home town.

"Are you going to open a restaurant?" we asked.

"If I do that and it's all about the money, I might as well have stayed in Leicester. I've come back for the lifestyle."

Hadrian had recognised what so many of us in Britain never grasp, as we slog away relentlessly with the longest working hours in Europe: the point at which he had enough.

When we asked about it, Hadrian showed us a picture of the castle in the 1920s, with its roof still intact. The village had been offered money to restore the castle, but had turned it down. Hadrian explained why.

"It would have ruined it. I have seen some of the 'restorations', like at Rupea. There's a car park right in front of the castle, huge lightning conductors on top and they poured in concrete to restore the stonework. I would like Saschiz to be restored the way you do it in the UK; preserving the ruins as they are, not creating some awful reconstruction."

Hadrian was raising money to organise a more conservative restoration of the castle. It was inspiring to hear his plans as he served us with freshly-pressed apple juice from his own trees.

"Do you want any water in it? This is a little less sweet from the summer apples. In autumn, it is very sweet."

Refreshed and rehydrated, we yearned for caffeine.

Hadrian suggested a 'Cold Brew'. This was a new one on us; cold brewed coffee.

"You grind the coffee on the largest setting, then soak it in cold water in the fridge for 24-hours. It is served on ice with tonic water and a twist of orange."

It was awesome.

We had another one.

Hadrian also stocked that quintessentially English drink, 'hand-picked elderflower cordial'. You can buy it in Waitrose.

"There's a factory here," he told us. "They pick the elderflowers on the river, just up there."

By the time we had finished our restorative relax and chat in the tranquil shade of Hadrian's place, it was 3.30pm and we were a touch behind schedule. On our way back to the UNESCO church at Buneşti, we passed several magical, little, hobbit villages, each with its own fortified church.

A sign informed us that we were only 8km from the World Heritage village of Viscri; it seemed rude not to. I was looking forward to visiting Viscri – one of 8,000 villages saved from Ceauşescu's bulldozers, along with Sângeorgiu de Pădure, which I mention because you know someone who came from there.

Sângeorgiu de Pădure was the birthplace of Claudine Rhédey. You remember Claudine. She is the Great-Great-Grandmother of Her Majesty Queen Elizabeth II – and the reason that the British Royal Family has vampire connections. Through Claudine, Prince

Charles is a great-grandson,16-times removed of Vlad Țepeș, fondly known as Dracula.

"The genealogy shows I am descended from Vlad the Impaler, so I do have a bit of a stake in the country," joked Charles in Charlie Ottley's wonderful documentary *Wild Carpathia*.

Thank goodness that he does; these royal connections were a critical factor in saving Sângeorgiu de Pădure, along with a host of other Romanian treasures.

A habit of failing to get to Viscri was beginning to develop, (we had planned to go yesterday!) At an incomprehensible sign in Romanian, we turned and, a mile further on, found a large digger blocking the road. We surmised that the sign had said 'Road Closed'. Since it was a long diversion to approach from the other direction and Viscri was do-able from our next campsite, we elected to uphold our fail consistency.

Blade had coped much better in the van. He was more settled – and didn't vomit, which was a plus. It had been a relatively short journey and, had it gone to plan, would have consisted of several hops and stops, which would have been good practice for him.

In general, Blade preferred to be outside, coming indoors only at bedtime. That evening, he asked to join us in the caravan. He lay down quietly and was as good as gold.

26

BIERTAN & ALMA VII

Dogs behaving badly, The Hunger Games & The Legend of Alma Vii

After conking out at around 8pm the previous night, it was to be expected that Blade was wide awake at 6:15am.

He brought this to our attention by repeatedly jumping up onto the bed.

"Blade. Off."

"Off."

"Off," I commanded, approximately once every fifteen seconds.

Finally, I gave in. He came on the bed for a brief cuddle, but then he started bouncing around and crawling over me, trying to reach Mark. We put him outside but he started barking immediately. To avoid waking the whole campsite, we gave in, got up – and decided to do breakfast again. Back at Casa Krauss, we met two Romanian girls and an English chap from Stockholm, "The most beautiful city in the world!"

"We're planning to go there next year."

"Save up for that one! Although in Sweden, there is *Allemansrätt* – 'Everyman's Right'. You can roam and camp anywhere, except in people's gardens; although perhaps not with a caravan."

Like every other person we had met, he had fallen in love with Romania.

The girls were an actress and a student doctor from Timişoara. They were exceptionally bright and confirmed one of Hadrian's points from yesterday,

"The last government was really good, but now we have a bad government. We thought that the previous government would definitely get in again, so we didn't vote... Romania still has its problems, but the next generation will change things. The older generation hankers after the communist era. There was no freedom and nothing in the shops, but things were easy. Everything was decided for you. The state 'looked after' you."

Unfortunately, 25 per cent of Romania's brightest left when communism ended. Thankfully, like Hadrian, a few are now returning and bringing with them both money and expertise. Part of the problem, the girls said, was one of aspiration.

"There is poverty here, but people with two cars and four TVs they think that they are poor. They think that 'not poor' is 'excess' – like America."

It brought to mind John Steinbeck's starkly

prophetic comments in which he stated that humans can cope with absolutely anything except abundance. Steinbeck asserted that the quickest and easiest way to destroy a nation is to render it sick, greedy and weak by giving it too much.

...

After breakfast, we went on to the World Heritage Fortified Church at Biertan. It was crowded and commercial; we were directed to park among the coaches and charged 10 lei (£2) for the privilege. However, it was stunning.

It stood out in the landscape, perched commandingly on top of a hill, with towers punctuating three tiers of 30ft-high defensive walls. Biertan is the largest medieval stronghold in Transylvania and had, unsurprisingly, proved impregnable. We walked around the base and wandered away from the commercial centre, straight into the extreme poverty and dirt roads of the village proper.

It was a considerable contrast. I was furious with Rosie, Lani and Ruby, who chased a chicken in the street. They didn't hurt it but they ignored our calls. A lady caught the chicken and allowed it to escape; I just hoped that it wouldn't die of a heart attack.

Mortified, we apologised profusely to the crowd who had now gathered. The dogs had been nose-to-beak with baby seagulls or incompetent fledglings and just sniffed them, but the chicken ran and the pups chase anything that moves. Nobody said a word of admonishment. They accepted our apology gracefully and then went quietly about their business. Who could say whether they were sharing our thoughts: 'Bloody tourists.'

The church was closed between 1 and 2pm, which saved us the 10 lei entrance fee. Dogs had to wait outside, so we took turns to ascend the covered, wooden walkway and admire the fortifications. The views were superb. I climbed one of the towers and looked out over the terracotta rooftops to the green, terraced hills of the countryside beyond. Biertan is part of a Natura 2000 natural protected area, Hârtibaciu-Târnava Mare. Natura 2000 is the largest ecological network in the world. Many footpaths and trails criss-cross through the quaint villages and wild-flower meadows of this incredible landscape. So, when we come back...

I spoke to a Dutchman, who had visited Romania eighteen times since 1990. He laughed at the horror stories that we had been fed before we came. Such tales are, it seems, exceedingly common – and categorically untrue. A bit like the Dracula legend of Vlad the Impaler.

A restaurant by the castle tempted us – we were set on stuffed cabbage rolls, a delicacy which boasts its own festival in Praid. The 45-minute wait for food precluded our staying; as usual, we had spent much longer than intended on our visit. Alternatives were limited; a cake shop, two bars and a village shop with a healthy stock of watermelons but little else, so we elected to push on.

Hunger was beginning to permeate all of my memories of Romania. Campsites rarely offered a bread service and finding somewhere to buy lunch was never a given. Shops had limited stock and the bread for sale was sometimes already mouldy.

A few miles on, we found a village shop. It was an education. It stocked no biscuits, no sandwiches and very few soft drinks. Mark returned with a selection of its finest: a packet of peanuts, a bag of Romanian Wotsits and two cans of Fanta. It cost the equivalent of £1.40. The shop had no money in the till, so Mark's change came as two boxes of matches.

It is worth mentioning here that we had stopped at pet shops in Mediaș and Sighișoara, both largeish towns, to try to buy a replacement for Blade's chewed lead. The pet shops were both about half the size of a small kitchen and offered only a miniscule amount of dog food. My guess is that holding stock was too expensive and that there was insufficient demand to carry a wide range of products. People selling watermelons at the roadside had been a common sight. If that could provide a living, perhaps a shop made you the Romanian equivalent of Alan Sugar.

...

The road to Alma Vii was rough; probably just tarmac laid on cobbles. You can't visit Alma Vii by accident. It is at the very end of a country road that winds for miles through pristine fields and forest.

The strange name of Alma Vii (not Alma VII as I had thought) stems from the legend that Helma, a girl who lived nearby, was accused of committing an 'immoral act' and chased into a lake by a male mob. They left thinking that she had drowned, although Helma hid among the reeds and survived. Afraid to return home, she built a hut by the lake. The present-day village, among the vineyards and orchards on the site of her hut, is known as Alma Vii, or 'Helma's Vineyard'. The lake silted up long ago, but the area is still called 'Old Woare – Ancient Lake'.

The fortified church in Alma Vii is not UNESCO-listed, so it was deserted. It was clear that a lot of cash had been lavished on the collapsing towers, but we were heartened to see a sympathetic restoration.

This was our first encounter with the MET (Mihai Eminescu Trust). MET recognised that Alma Vii is a treasure; not only because of its Saxon houses, but its harmonious, ethnically diverse population and traditions that have continued for generations. MET's 'Whole Village Project' set out to preserve the customs and traditional farming practices along with the buildings. Their enlightened intervention trained locals in masonry, carpentry and agritourism and taught them to speak English.

MET empowered the local people to repair the many ancient, wooden bridges on the pathways to their houses and to pave the village roads with rocks from the river. Each house is painted in bright, traditional colours and bears the family crest. With a traditional guesthouse or two thrown into the mix, Alma Vii has been conserved not just as a dry, museum piece, but as something much more authentic and beautiful – a living village. Here, the centuries-old lifestyle is not only alive but thriving – and brings with it something much more precious. Something which, in our quest for ever greater material wealth, we have either lost, forgotten or dismissed as unimportant; a sense of community.

...

Eat, Play, Love – A Letter from Blade

They told me that there is a lovely fur-ever home waiting for me in England and that's why I can't go on the bed. The Frou Frou dogs sleep there, but English humans don't all like dogs on the bed so I gotta learn. They want the Frou Frous to have their own 'space' too, cuz they are boring and don't want to play with me 24-hours a day.

I got told off for jumping on the bed while they were all in there. It was after 6am – everyone is up by then! I thought that they were all dead, so I bounced on them. They got a bit cross, then they all died again. I got worried, so I bounced on them again. Then they all died again...

27

CAMPSITE DE OUDE WILG, CÂRŢA

Romani Reflections

6:40am; Blade awoke. We hatched a cunning plan; an early breakfast sent him back to sleep.

He would not have slept without Mark sitting with him on the sofa, but the Blade-free zone granted the puppies and me a glorious, luxurious lie in until a record 10am. Many dog owners tell us that their dogs get them up at stupid-o'clock. In contrast, The Fab Four possess the sleep habits of students. If we didn't get them up, they would still be in bed at 4pm watching *Countdown*.

The early breakfast was also intended to address the issue of Blade vomiting in the van, although two factors conspired against us on this.

Naffsat routed us on what were shown as yellow roads in our atlas; A-roads in Romania but loosely equivalent to British B-roads. There was a shorter route via what the map showed as white, Romanian B-roads, although we were now savvy enough to know that a white road could easily be a cornfield – or worse. Even so, the dreadful state of the yellow roads caused Blade to vomit.

The early breakfast had been a good idea on travelling day, although what I emptied out of my sandal was probably Blade's hooverings of the remains from the puppies' 10am breakfast. That said, Blade was better in the van. He did lie down and relax eventually. The panting, yawning and salivating had stopped – if only we could get there with the vomiting.

The poverty that we saw en route was humbling. In one village, a horse and cart waited outside a hovel, afloat in a sea of mud, with a bed sheet for a front door.

...

Our new campsite, 'De Oude Wilg' in the village of Cârța, was lovely; a green oasis, shaded with fruit trees. As we checked in, the owner gave us each a small, tasting-bottle of home-made raspberry liqueur. It made a delicious toast to our new home.

Walking the dogs from the campsite, Mark met a beautifully dressed Roma lady. She asked for food for her children. After the poverty that we had seen, it touched both of our hearts. We needed supplies, so Mark bought her a full bag of shopping on his trip to Lidl in Făgăraș.

"Remember that they might not have a fridge," I called after him.

The lady wasn't around when he got back, so we asked the campsite owner where we might find her.

"I wish you hadn't bought her anything. They have everything they need – and they could lend *you* money! The Roma just don't want to work. I have loads to do on the campsite, but I can't get help. I don't like them pestering guests."

It was a lesson learned; we reassured him that we hadn't handed over the shopping. We could use the toothpaste, shower gel, vitamins and tinned vegetables. Undoubtedly, Blade would help with the jars of baby food.

...

It is impossible to write about Romania without mentioning the Roma or Romani, the country's largest ethnic minority.

The issue of the Roma is a complicated one and we could only take charity guidance from a local. Roma wealth and their approach to work did seem to vary considerably. We thought back to the ostentation of the golden-gated mansions that we had passed just after crossing into Romania, although those contrasted markedly with the glaring poverty of the majority of Roma communities that we had seen.

Originally thought to be from northern India, Roma gypsies have lived in Europe for more than 1,500

years. Sadly, their long and varied history has been
defined by one single constant – persecution.
Hundreds of thousands of Roma were kept as slaves in
Romania. A largely unknown statistic from the Holo-
caust is that, alongside Jews, homosexuals and the
handicapped, over half a million Roma were extermi-
nated in Nazi death camps.

From the 1970s to 1990 in Czechoslovakia, Roma
women were forcibly sterilised and even more shock-
ingly, the Far Right in other countries is keen to re-
introduce this inhuman initiative. In 2013, influential
Hungarian journalist Zsolt Bayer called for a 'final
solution' – referring to the Roma as 'animals' who
'shouldn't be allowed to exist'. Even the term 'gypsy'
was, for many years, a label as offensive and derogatory
as the now taboo words used to describe other ethnic
groups. ('Gypsy' arose from Europeans mistaking
Roma for Egyptians – 'gyptians'. 'Rom' has nothing to
do with Romania; it is the Romani word for 'Man',
derived from the Sanskrit 'Dom'.)

Although many are now settled, often in abandoned Saxon homes, Roma were traditionally a travelling people. Different branches of Roma were skilled
as metal-workers, livestock traders, healers, enter-
tainers and musicians. Roma views on what is important in life differ markedly from those of Western
Europeans. Roma do value a higher degree of leisure
and family time over work – but who can blame them?
Certainly not Mark and I, since we have chosen the
same path. The difference was that we had opted for a

more relaxed lifestyle only after suffering ill-health, caused by the stress and long hours of our supposedly advanced and civilised Western way of life.

Roma are often criticised for keeping their children out of school. Yet Roma consider children so precious that families can't bear to be apart, even for a day. (We feel the same way about our Fur Babies!) Nannies, nurseries, boarding schools, after-school clubs and summer camps; perhaps I agree with the Roma. I have often wondered why anyone would farm out the critical job of bringing up their kids to total strangers. Understandably, the Roma also harbour a strong suspicion about government influence on young minds and, of course, school equates to bullying, due to deeply ingrained racism.

Whatever the rights and wrongs of their approach to an acceptable work-life balance, the Roma remain entrapped in a Catch-22 of prejudice. It keeps 75 per cent of European Roma below the poverty line and seriously limits their choices. Undoubtedly, there is a degree of criminality associated with Roma communities, although this is often exaggerated. Everybody knows that the Roma abduct children – except that this is not true. There is *absolutely zero* documentary evidence to support this popular myth. However, if you are denied jobs and opportunities, crime and begging are an inevitable and unsurprising consequence.

Anti-Semitism, homophobia, disability discrimination and attitudes to many other marginalised groups have been recognised and are improving. Sadly, the

Roma remain among the most persecuted minorities in Europe.

It is for everyone to make up their own minds, but the issue of the Roma does seem to result from a clash of substantially different cultures. When Mark and I analysed our views, we had to ask ourselves, "Is it right for us to judge the Roma by our Western values and standards?" And the West is always happy to find some bogeymen to blame for everything.

Our Roma lady may not have been one of those in dire need, but I began to see things a little from her point of view. We were wealthy and well-fed. She wanted an easy life and time with her children. If we were willing to make a donation, why not?

28

FĂGĂRAȘ & SÂMBĂTA DE JOS

*The Fabulous Fortress of Făgăraș & the Largest Herd of
Lipizzaners in Romania*

If there are horses to be found, you know that I would
find them. And if there is the largest herd of Lipizzaners in Romania, you know that I would have to go
there – and 'there' just happened to be up the road in
Sâmbăta de Jos.

The welcome was as warm as at Lipica, although
the stud could not have been more different. A dilapidated mansion house greeted us as we entered the
gates. The long, low stable block to the right was run-
down and certainly lacked the majesty and scrubbed
cleanliness of Lipica. However, both places contained
the same, delicious, warm scent of horse, motes of dust
dancing in sunlight that beamed through the high
windows and the contented sound of hay being
munched.

Dogs were welcome everywhere except inside the stable, which was home to fifty stallions; all from the seven foundation blood lines. I left Mark and the pack outside as I went in to meet one of the old boys, Conversano XXXV 1998. He nuzzled me gently over the door of his loose box as I scratched behind his ears. A row of rumps stretched the full length of the building. Many of the stallions were lined up in stalls; 'stallion' does mean 'stalled one.' I was wary, wandering behind all those back feet. The boys had kicked many holes in the plywood dividers. It pays to remember that stallions are beautiful, but feisty – aside from dressage, teeth and heels are two fundamental reasons why stallions were used for hundreds of years as a weapon of war.

When our guide told us that the starting price for a Romanian Lipizzaner was €3,000, Mark and I shared the same thought, "Would Maestoso LIII 2006 and a pal fit in a caravan with five dogs?!"

...

Moving on to the 14th century citadel of Făgăraş was not too shabby. The huge, gilded dome of the Cathedral of John the Baptist was visible from miles away, shimmering in the sunshine. Later, along with weeping willows, we saw it reflected in the still, blue waters of the moat that surrounded the formidable, terracotta-coloured curtain walls of the fortress. As we wandered along the moat's grassy banks, we warned

Rosie not to mess with the swans who had made their home there. Especially the jet-black, vampire swans.

It was Transylvania, so naturally there were vampire connections in Făgăraş. The Black Tower of the medieval fortress was built by some ruler of Walachia, that bloke Vlad III.

Only one bridge spanned the moat. The pups were allowed to join us inside the fortress, but could not enter the rooms or museum unless carried. The lady at the kiosk was extremely accommodating, but did grin as she observed that it would be difficult to carry five dogs. We agreed that we would go inside one at a time and meanwhile, she took a selfie with The Famous Five.

Once again, after a tough program of sightseeing, I was ravenous, but since we were in a town, I did rate my chances of scoring a snack. What I hadn't factored into the equation was that fast food does not exist in Romania. After a wait of over forty minutes, even Kai had given up hope of ever seeing that fried chicken sandwich.

29

BLADE'S BIG DAY

From Lost Boy to Loved Boy - An Officially Adopted Orphan

It was official.

Our Transylvanian Orphan now had a legitimate family as well as documents for international travel.

Once again, the vet in Cisnădie had been excused from hospital duty, so we had an early-morning appointment for Blade's final check-up, after which the vet would issue his passport. Our dawn drive was enchanting; the sun cast a faint, silvery-yellow light over the pale grey Carpathian Mountains to our left and lit up gossamer swathes of mist, draped tastefully across the Transylvanian plain.

Holding Blade's passport felt like a lottery win. The vet posed for a photo and urged us to send him email updates on Blade's progress. He liked Blade's name.

"As in the film!" he said, delightedly.

We hit Cisnădie for a celebratory coffee. It is a wonderful village, bustling with life on a weekday morning. Pavement cafés fringed the pretty, cobbled square, overlooked by the solid presence of the 200ft clock tower within the walls of the fortified church, which was one of my favourites. The 12th-century Romanesque basilica is beautiful, however the sheer bulk of the surrounding Saxon fortifications, added in the 15th century, contributed a solid sense of permanence that was nothing less than profound.

Inside the sanctuary and inner sanctuary of the concentric, defensive walls were colourful gardens, alive with flowers. A spectacular, covered, wooden walkway ran around the inside of the whitewashed perimeter wall. We savoured the brooding atmosphere since, of course, we had it all to ourselves.

Leaving the church through the heavy, wooden gate, studded and criss-crossed with iron, felt like a metaphor for Blade stepping through a door into his new life.

...

Maybe it was the sudden peace of mind derived from being officially adopted. Viscri had been the plan. Definitely the plan. Except that Blade allowed us a lie in.

It was late when we got up, so instead, we decided

to walk into the village of Cârța to see the fortified church and monastery. We also wanted to try to find a footpath to the river so that we could burn off a little doggie steam before we met our nemesis and tackled the Transfăgărașan with Kismet. A group of grumpy English campers tried to put our already angst-ridden minds to rest by telling us that it was snowing on the summit and we'd never make it.

It was a lovely, warm September day; about 25°C with a little breeze. It felt so wonderful after the blazing heat of a Transylvanian August. A beautifully dressed wedding party who lined the street outside the impressive ruins of the monastery shared smiles and waves with us.

We failed to find the footpath along the river and had failed to remember our money to pay 5 lei (£1) to go into the fortified church. On our way home, we struck up a conversation with a local, who was fixing the kerb outside his gate. He introduced himself as Cristian.

"I have to fix my own kerb because I can't get help."

We chatted for a while before he invited us in for a glass of home-made elderflower cordial. As we chilled in the shade of his rampantly green garden, he told us:

"I lived in Canada for thirty years, but I am a rebel and got disillusioned with the system. They say you have freedom; but you don't, so I came back. You can hide in Romania."

It's true. In the West, infinite choice gives an illusion of freedom. We can buy anything we want, so long as it is from M&S, Next, Sainsbury's – all the same shops in every town. All owned by the same, few – but hugely powerful – global corporations.

But global corporations will catch you eventually, wherever you are. On our way back from Cisnădie with Blade the previous day, we had visited the huge shopping mall in Sibiu and had Kentucky Fried Chicken for lunch.

...

Eat, Play, Love – A Letter from Blade

I now have an official birthday written on a passport. 1st January, the same as racehorses, they said.

They gave me toys and laughed because I played with the boxes "Just like all kids!" They didn't laugh so much when I played with their shoes. OK, I ate their shoes. But it was a great game.

The Dogfather and Dogmother have changed sides. On the bed, I mean. They haven't defected to a rogue state. (At least I hope not. I did hear them discussing the Battle of the Bed.) The Dogfather is more difficult to jump over, but I only get up there to make sure that everyone is comfortable. I really care about my new family. If I didn't, I wouldn't need to check so often, would I?

The Dogmother likes the new arrangement because the Dogfather has to make the coffee in the morning and she's next to the loo. I know not to poo inside but they do all the time. They keep it in a box! Then, when I poo on a nice, high tree stump so that everyone knows that I'm around, they collect it in a bag and store that in a box. What do they want it for?

30

THE PRINCE OF WALES AND THE WEISSKIRCH

Cincşor - & finally - Viscri

We slewed into the car park at the fortified church at Cincşor, just after the very pleasingly named town of 'Voila'.

It was a last-minute decision; we were just passing, but it was a superb idea. Like so many of the 'lesser' churches (non-UNESCO) it was beautiful. We climbed up towers that would give 'Elf and Safety' a field day – we had to watch where we put our feet to avoid taking the quick way back to the ground, straight through the floor.

The lady curator welcomed us in, pups and all. There were two dogs in the churchyard anyway, one sleeping quietly among the flowers. When we had finished our tour, the bigger one, Rex, blocked the door to try to prevent his five new playmates from leaving.

Blade had achieved many things in the previous

ten days. In Cincşor he mastered the most important: The Solo Puppy Pose. He sat and stayed like a pro all on his own as I photographed him among the blooms.

...

Then, at last, we moved on to Viscri.

Isolated and inaccessible, down a long, rough road, the 12th-century Saxon village of Viscri has been held in a time warp. Like Alma Vii, both the buildings and traditions had been subjected to the sympathetic and holistic intervention of MET. Former patron, Charles, The Prince of Wales, had visited Viscri and fallen for her, saying:

"Do not change anything. Keep and love this place as it is."

Charles bought a house in Viscri, which is now operated as a guest house. Local crafts are encouraged; bricks, tiles and metalwork are all made in the village. Through 'The Sock Project', local women knit thousands of natural woollen products, which are sold locally and exported to Germany. Stalls selling brightly-coloured knitwear lined the cobbled street leading up to the UNESCO designated fortified church.

Given the title 'Alba Ecclesia' or 'White Church' (*Weißkirch* in Saxon/German), it is deemed one of the best in Transylvania. It was lovely and undoubtedly interesting architecturally; unusual in having been built around an existing Szekler chapel. (The Szeklers, a Turkic tribe, were early settlers.) However, it was not my favourite. And the large, tourist coaches parked in the centre of town did nothing to add to the peace or historical ambience.

Once again, I was starving. Lured in by the picnic tables, umbrellas and chairs sitting invitingly outside, we stopped at what appeared to be the only lunch opportunity in Viscri, a *Magazin Mixt* – 'Mixed Shop' on the main street. A pot of paint was no problem, but a sandwich at lunchtime was out of the question. The large, shapeless, beige owner, sitting in a large, shapeless, beige armchair inside seemed put out at having to serve me. After lengthy consideration of her eclectic range of stock, I interrupted her knitting to purchase the best she had to offer: two pre-packed, chocolate croissants and a bag of chicken-flavoured crisps.

I smelled the coffee before I spotted the machine. I asked for two coffees with milk. Via the medium of mime, she expressed the possibility as "no chance". I indicated that I would get a soft drink instead, but as I was cogitating a cornucopia of carbonated cans, trying to decide which I disliked the least, she shot out of her armchair. She had suddenly called to mind something long forgotten. As she bent down low, her skirts rode high to reveal bulky, thick-stockinged legs as she rummaged in the back of a fridge full of animal parts. You might think that I am joking, but there was a jumble of hind legs and cloven hooves in there. As she straightened up, she was holding a grubby, grey, plastic milk container, half filled with what looked like curds and whey. She made two coffees and, thankfully, put the milk in a jug, since it exuded the aroma of a well-ripened Camembert.

As I settled with Mark and the dogs at a table outside, she seemed to get agitated. Her disquiet revolved around an etiolated, dwarf tomato plant growing next to the leg of the picnic table.

"Kaput," she kept repeating, indicating the plant and gesticulating in horror at the dogs.

Had it been possible to purchase lunch in the shop, I would have said that the plant had self-seeded from a cheese and tomato sandwich. However, to preserve her precious plant and its crop of a single, pale cherry tomato, we moved to another table and ate our plastic croissant. We opted to drink our coffee black. At least our lunchtime treat cost only 14 lei – just under £3 – and as a bonus, it gave Mark and me a subject for lunchtime conversation.

"What's *wrong* with this country? A café here would be a goldmine!"

Had I not been so ravenous that I had single-mindedly pursued the first and seemingly only food option, a walk around the village would have revealed a café, a bakery and a proper restaurant with a menu and everything. Unfortunately, by the time we found the café in the mid-afternoon, it was closing and when we stumbled upon the restaurant, it was time to depart in respect of doggie dinner-time.

We followed the hordes processing up to the fortified church. Everywhere inside, signs dictated that photos were permitted for personal use only; bad news for a blogger. Inside the church, we discovered a fine example of Romanian pragmatism; falling asleep in church was not a crime, but you could be fined if the second person along could hear you snoring.

The WWI memorial plaques on the church wall were extremely moving. Many of the dead shared exactly the same name – both first and second names. Numbers appeared after each name; clearly not their age, since they ran into the hundreds. Their Regiments, perhaps?

The lovely lady on the door explained,

"They are all cousins, who share the same family names. Those are their house numbers in the village."

That made it extremely personal.

The lady pointed out where we could walk the dogs in the countryside surrounding Viscri. A picturesque stroll up the village took us past a second church and into the woods. We circled back when we met some sheep with their shepherd dogs (Romanian shepherd dogs are notoriously ferocious and best avoided!). The meadows around the village had commanding views over the village. Like most monuments, Viscri looked amazing from the outside. Blade went off lead for the first time in the open and nailed it. His recall rivalled that of a champion obedience dog at Crufts.

A gypsy horse and cart accompanied us as we wandered back into the village. A small child on board grinned broadly at the pups,

"De vanzare? – For Sale?"

"Non vanzare!" I replied with conviction and an even broader grin. Not for a million pounds each.

Driving back, we were captivated by the commanding hilltop fortress at Rupea, one of the oldest archaeological sites in Romania. With evidence of human settlement dating back to the Palaeolithic era, the Saxon citadel was built on an earlier Dacian fortress. Rupea is reputedly where the defeated Dacian king, Decebal, committed suicide to avoid capture by the Romans.

As we drove back into Cârța, a strange, stormy light backlit the Carpathian Mountains, which looked dark and threatening. My nerves were jangling. The following day, with Kismet in tow, we were going in.

31

TOWING THE TRANSFĂGĂRĂȘAN – CROSSING THE CARPATHIANS WITH A CARAVAN

The Winding Way to Walachia

We had received little encouragement about driving over the Transfăgărășan with the caravan. Besides telling us that we would drive straight into a blizzard on the summit, the miserable Brits had no confidence that Big Blue was even capable of getting Kismet up there. They piled on the pressure by asking, "Do you have extra coolant and a spare belt?"

I tried to console myself that the Transfăgărășan had been built for military vehicles. The maximum gradient was 11 per cent for a short stretch; the Vršič pass in Slovenia was 14 per cent which gave me a reference. Ever the optimist, Mark made a promise:

"It'll be a piece of cake."

Nevertheless, I can't say that I departed our campsite in Cârța without trepidation. A band of German bikers with big beards had camped next to us. They competed annually in the Isle of Man T.T. race. They seemed dubious about our chances of hauling Kismet over the Transfăgărăşan.

"We rode it yesterday. The surface is not good. It is very steep and very narrow. You will have to watch that you don't, how you say? Catch the back. Ground out."

This from perennial risk-takers, who put their lives on the line by hurling themselves around the Manx circuit at 150mph in 'the most dangerous race in the world'.

"We're planning to drive over the Transfăgărăşan," I told the lady owner as I paid her for the campsite.

I scanned her face for any flicker of reaction or doubt. There was none. I suspect that she had long since lost interest in the hair-brained schemes of tourists.

Our stop at Lidl in Făgăras on the way back yesterday had highlighted that Sunday night was not the best time to seek full supermarket shelves. We had no onions. In addition, we had forgotten to get cash, fill up with fuel and check our tyres, water and oil. After all, we had 56 miles to do, 6,699ft to climb and a few twists and turns to navigate.

Rather than wasting valuable time by making a sensible trip back to Făgăras with nothing in tow, we hit the road. I kept a lookout for somewhere promising to stop for money and supplies. In Victoria, we circled the town centre before finding a supermarket car park large enough to accommodate a caravan. There is nothing like a view of cancerous communist concrete opposite a Lidl to start a scary day. As I waited for Mark, I thoroughly enjoyed the irony of seeing a horse and cart trot past the now crumbling image of Ceaușescu's 'modern' Romania.

Big Blue and Kismet climbed through the beautiful Transylvanian forests towards mountain peaks topped by cloud. Looks of open-mouthed wonder as we passed did nothing to reassure us that we had made the right decision.

As we emerged above the tree line, we were faced by a huge waterfall, crashing hundreds of feet down the immense, solid, rock wall at the head of the valley.

"We're going up *there*?" Mark asked in disbelief.

It looked like it. Literally, the only way was up.

The road snaked around the mountainside and did indeed, come out at the top of the cascade. We halted on a precipice to take photos. Our views back to the sparkling plain of Transylvania, far below, twinkled with a glimmer of magic.

Above the tree line, we could see the road winding upwards through bleak mountain scenery. Now, we were entering an uncompromising world of rocks, mist and cloud.

I have mentioned Romanian driving habits before, but on the Transfăgărășan, they abandoned all the rules of Romania Mania. Even though the road was narrow, uphill and had a steep drop to the side (with no barriers), not one person overtook on blind bend with a lorry coming the other way. Not once were we forced to brake sharply to ensure that no-one died.

The Transfăgărășan is evidently a road that commands respect – and reverential adherence to the 40km speed limit, even among Romanians.

We pulled over to get photographic evidence of Big Blue and Kismet on the hairpins. This was just below Bâlea Lake, the high point of the Transfăgărășan. Bâlea is a glacial lake; one of Romania's 'must-see' natural wonders. There are cafés. It was mobbed. We didn't stop

The Transfăgărășan was commercial, with plenty of eateries along the route. However, this was still Romania. At no point was I confident that I would not cross the Carpathians starving as well as scared.

At Conacul Ursului, we stopped for a coffee and cake. It was a large café with plenty of seating outside. It was charmingly Romanian.

"Please can we order some food and coffee?"

"No."

"Oh."

"We have a group in. We can't do food." (The group was already tucking in to a pre-prepared buffet.)

"Well, could we have just a coffee?"

"*Sigh*. I suppose."

"And a cake?"

"No."

Coffee was grudgingly produced with a tiny plastic carton of milk.

We had no stopover planned for the night, but had noticed a campsite next door. There were also appealing signs for potential doggie-walks along the river in the dark-green forest.

"What's the situation with the campsite next door?"

"I don't know. This is just the hotel. My neighbour runs the campsite."

"There is nobody there. Do you know who I ask?"

"No."

I was just glad that Mark had been sensible enough to bank two emergency pasties in Lidl, Victoria. Otherwise, even on this trip – with its seemingly plentiful refreshment stops – I would have been subjected to the shakes from low blood sugar, never mind the sheer drops.

We pushed on and decided to miss out a few of our planned stops to make more headway. The road twisted for miles along the crenellated edge of the Vidraru lake, whose azure waters winked and glistened in the sun between the trees. Of course, there was no way down and no footpaths along the shoreline. At the Vidraru Dam, there was a car park, so we stopped to give the dogs a leg-stretch.

The dam on the Argeş River was built in the mid-1960s to create Lake Vidraru. To give passers-by a clue to its purpose, an immense, silver sculpture of Prometheus, holding aloft a bolt of lightning, was perched on a rocky crag above the dam, looking for all the world like a Marvel Superhero.

It's hydroelectricity. In case you didn't guess. In Greek Mythology, Prometheus stole fire from the gods and gave it to us mortals.

As we continued, we passed a flock of sheep being driven by six tall, rangy dogs. Of course, a 6 vs 5 bark-off quickly developed. I put the camera out of the van window and tried, but failed, to get the money shot: a photograph of the caravan being chased up the road by six monstrous and moderately outraged Romanian shepherd dogs.

What goes up must come down – and down... The descent from Transylvania into Walachia was spectacular. We dropped into deep gorges, where we could look back up to the road that we had driven, to see soaring viaducts, spanning steep chasms. There are 830 bridges and 27 viaducts on the Transfăgărașan, although I didn't count.

All of a sudden, a fantastic hilltop castle hove into view – and a sign which announced 'Dracula Camping'. Poienari castle had been on our list of sights to see, but we had given up on it. Our web-research had been definitive – there were absolutely no campsites anywhere nearby. We drew quickly into a layby opposite the very real and existing campsite, which was located directly under the castle. The campsite reception housed the castle's entrance kiosk.

Poienari was a castle where Vlad definitely woz 'ere. At Bran, of course, 'e wozn't at all; not that the tourist industry would let historical accuracy inhibit a Dracula goldmine.

Two or three mangy strays wandered around the campsite. Dr Doolittle struck again; Mark provided a beef and salmon dinner for everybody plus a bandaged paw for one poor little pooch, who was limping badly.

We were wary of our neighbours. The campsite had a high perimeter fence, bearing abundant portraits of the locals. Head-shots of snarling grizzlies led us to place the small can of bear spray that Jake had given us strategically inside the caravan. We also emptied the bin on the inside of our Alu-tech caravan door, which now looked far too flimsy to be bear-proof.

Mark had promised that towing the Transfăgărășan would be a piece of cake. It had not been, but that was only due to the quirks of Romanian cafés. Aside from a slightly smelly clutch and a further addition to the grimy fan of oil droplets sprayed down Kismet's side, it was conclusively Caravan 1, Carpathians 0.

32

POENARI – VLAD'S PAD IS CLOSED

Slowly, We Come Around to the Benefits of an Armed Escort

The plan was to pack up, pop up to Drac's castle and then depart. Blade needed exercise; 1,480 steps seemed just the ticket. We got the caravan ready to roll, then the woman on the turnstile told us:

"The castle is closed."

"The sign says it's open from 10 until 3."

"No. It's open at 10 *and* 3."

"Why? It's just a path up to a ruined castle; there's no guided tour."

"There's a bear with two cubs up there. At 10 and 3 my colleague goes up with two armed policemen."

OK. *That* seemed like a good enough reason.

We booked another night – and felt a new gratitude for the electric fence around the campsite, which we christened the Bear Grills. At this point, we didn't realise quite how much more gratitude we might feel a few hours later.

...

Everybody knows that bears have an excellent sense of smell and that the sure-fire way to attract a bear is to leave out food. We had taken this seriously enough to empty the bin on the inside of the caravan door. It would be reasonable to ask, then:

"Why did you go to bed in bear country with a plate of bread and butter on your caravan roof?"

Bread was a rarity. The campsite café/shop/reception sold no food, so we had made a ham sandwich with the remnants of a three-day old loaf. It was horrible. After picking out the more edible bits, we left the rest on a plate. We didn't put the remnants in the bin; we were being careful about that, because of the bears, but we needed to place it beyond the reach of Blade.

"I'll put the plate on the roof," Mark announced. "To keep it out of the way."

"We'd better not forget about that!" I joked.

We forgot about it. Then went for a siesta.

...

Since the sandwich was so disappointing and lunch at the campsite was out of the question, we treated ourselves at the Cetate restaurant, just down the road. They welcomed the dogs, then served us with goulash and the best papanași yet.

At 3pm, we mustered with our armed guard and, powered by papanași, prepared to face 1,480 steps. The smokers fell by the wayside at the first bend. The staying power of the bloke wearing the T-shirt stating "Party at Mine!" was disappointing. He would never have made dawn.

On a plateau of Mount Cetetea, only a few walls and ramparts remain. Abandoned in the 1500s, the structure was damaged further by an earthquake in 1888. Poenari has a long and chequered history; constructed by Walachians in the 13th century, it changed hands a few times before falling into disrepair. High on a precipice and difficult to conquer, Vlad the Impaler spotted its potential and resurrected it as one of his principal fortresses.

It was a pretty, shady walk up through the forest and, as you would expect, the castle commanded fantastic views. Behind, the Argeș River glistened beneath the final, dramatic viaducts and bridges of the Transfăgărașan; ahead, it shimmered off into the lush, green distance.

There was little to show for Vlad's presence, other than a motley selection of mannequins, impaled on wooden poles. It seemed like a raw deal for a mannequin; swathed in Harrods' finest or impaled on a stake in a windswept ruin on a remote, Romanian hillside.

From within the walls, it was easy to imagine the

legends that surround Vlad; enjoying a banquet among a forest of impaled victims, who writhed in agony while he tucked into slices of bread dipped in their blood.

It is difficult for us to comprehend such cruelty, although in those troubled times, homicidal tendencies were probably much prized.

Like a metaphorical Bear Grills, murderous psychopathy was probably your best bet for survival.

33

THE SWISS CHEESE PARADOX

A Question of Chocolate, Cheese & Neutrality

Leaving Poenari, we took the scenic route towards Bran and Brașov through the mountains. The view was jaw-dropping at every turn – as were the potholes. The state of the carriageway suggested that the road had been surfaced with a super-sized waffle iron, prior to the careful addition of obstacles to keep the driver alert, such as randomly-angled show jumps or craters.

What is deceptive is that some of the bumps that you see turn out not to be so bad. Then you hit an invisible one and it propels you into orbit. We hit one of those.

Travelling at about 35mph, Mark saw the consequences unfold in the towing mirrors.

"All six wheels actually left the road! The caravan pivoted at the hitch – I saw it bend up then down. I'm sure that the back hit the deck."

We pulled over to check for damage. There was nothing visible. It was only when we reached the campsite and looked underneath that we discovered a crack spanning the full width of the caravan floor.

At a WWI memorial, we stopped in the hope of getting a restorative coffee. The car park was filled with stalls selling Dracula tat, of course, but no food or drink. The café was so closed that the last customer had probably been Vlad Țepeș himself. Mark fed a couple of strays. One was a cute, long-legged pup. We had to have a hard chat with ourselves so as not to pop him in the van with us. He would have had no problem finding a home; but six dogs? Two strays? In a caravan?

We could live with that, but seemingly not UK Customs.

Throngs of tourists were milling around Bran. I snapped the Dracula castle where Dracula never went (although Drac's dad was there for a while) out of the van window and saw a fountain with a tasteless cartoon vampire picked out in colourful mosaic.

"Don't worry about photos, we'll be back," Mark said, but as we contemplated the crowds and crawled through roadworks all the way to Râșnov, it became clear. Unlike Arnie, The Terminator, we would definitely not be back.

The vast, golden, hilltop fortress at Râșnov was imposing and impressive. We passed beneath it and drove a mile up a rocky, potholed road to the campsite, Cheile Râșnoavei, which sat by a stream with green hills behind.

"*Five dogs!*"

I initiated my speech to the lady at reception. "They're small and well behaved…"

"I *love* dogs," she interrupted me warmly, before directing us to a pitch which was near another small dog, but well away from a big dog.

Two smart, new motorhomes were parked nearby, so it was not long before we had a run-in with the Swiss. Our hearts had sunk when we saw CH on the number plates, just as they instantly soar whenever we see NL. Not that we have anything against the Swiss per se. We love their sadistic food – pleasure and pain moulded into a chocolate triangle that stabs the roof of your mouth; fondues that strip skin like napalm; £50 in a Geneva restaurant for two burgers that were slimy and inedible…

We haven't met many Swiss, so we can't claim a statistically sound sample. However, what we can say is that 100 per cent of the Swiss whom we have met have not been very friendly.

It had been a long and stressful drive. Blade had vomited over everyone. Pitching had not been easy; manoeuvring was tight and there wasn't one part of the area that was flat. Having been stuck in the car for hours, I was desperate for a cup of tea. I was wrestling 100ft of electricity cable, trying to unravel and connect it, deploying a range of adapters to correct for reverse polarity and a two-pin supply. Mark was beneath the caravan, inspecting the pothole-inflicted crack, which had riven the caravan floor, trying to assess whether it was BDT – Beyond Duct Tape. Spotting our distraction, Rosie took it upon herself to escape and embark on her own little quest to meet the neighbours.

For non-caravanners, I should explain that 100ft of heavy-duty electricity cable is quite weighty. It also has a mind of its own. Regardless of how neatly it is rolled on departure, even on a short journey, you will arrive to find that it has knitted itself into a bedspread. Engrossed in my cable conundrum, the first I knew of Rosie's impromptu diplomatic mission was:

"Do you hev a beg to pick up shit?"

First contact. From the Swiss. A complaint – and we hadn't even finished pitching.

She had caught me at a disadvantage; I was thrashing around in a shrubbery, bound by the tentacles of an orange, electrical Medusa. But before I had even uttered the word "Yes", never mind offered my sincere apology, I got:

"Eet ees very inconsiderate. Unacceptable. *Outrageous!*"

Like Harry Houdini, I wrestled my way out of the constricting curls of cable. I produced a poo bag straight out of my pocket and presented it like a magician, "Ta Dah!" to indicate my permanent state of preparedness to deal with shit. I tried to narrow things down by asking her to indicate the location.

All I got was "Inconsiderate. Unacceptable. *Outrageous!*" but repeated more loudly.

I had no option but to embark on a blind turd hunt around the Swiss section. She followed me too closely and maintained her verbal assault by leaning into my ear to shout:

"Eet is very Inconsiderate. Unacceptable. *Outrageous!*"

I am ashamed to say that my patience snapped. I rounded on her. She was short, fat and grey with a short, fat, grey attitude. The sort who likes to provoke people, then accuse them of being unreasonable. During my incoherent tirade, which centred around my having had enough and not being in the mood for this, I saw it in her eyes. She had won.

Her initial point was perfectly valid. It was careless of us not to spot our escapee – but with dozens of strays wandering freely around campsites, we had been less particular than usual over dog restraint. It had been a bad day. My tolerance for taking the rap for every irresponsible dog owner in the world had deserted me.

Remarkably, I located the turd and flounced off with as much dignity as an electrical cable-wrestler carrying a small bag of poo can muster.

Although a Swiss saying suggests that "It's easier to criticise than to do better", the lodging of a complaint was inevitable. We had been there before. Eviction loomed and we'd only just arrived. My heart plummeted.

We were on tenterhooks, trying to keep the dogs quiet and meticulously tethered. A kind man in a checked shirt came and helped me to whip my electricity cable into submission. By the bunch of keys on his hip, I deduced that he was from the campsite. He smiled at the dogs and when I tried to stop Blade from jumping up to say hello, he fussed him.

"It's fine," he reassured me.

But I couldn't relax. Every time a dog barked, even when it wasn't one of ours (the campsite was surrounded by strays) I winced and felt the size of the complaint growing malevolently, like a tumour.

A major plus in Romania had been the laid-back attitude in the campsites. No lists of rules. No petty Jobsworths. I had no doubt that unreasonable guest behaviour would not be tolerated, Romanian campsite owners are a hardy breed. However, in general, everything was relaxed – they genuinely did want everybody to enjoy their stay.

And the amazing result of this laissez-faire attitude was that treating people like adults tended to make them step up to the plate. We had experienced no problems with anyone, anywhere. No noise, no annoyance and no grumpy, self-appointed busybodies – until we met the Swiss.

Swiss cheese has lots of holes. The more cheese you have, the more holes you have. The more holes you have, the less cheese you have.

Thus, the more you have – the less you have. That is the Swiss Cheese Paradox.

Perhaps it explains a lot.

34

BRASSED OFF IN BRAȘOV – PART 1

The Black Church & The Bullets in the Wall

We were drawn to Brașov by the promise of Baroque and Saxon architecture, the Gothic 'Black Church' and the narrowest street in Europe.

Naffsat decided that the best and quickest route was nothing to do with driving directly there. It took us via Poiana Brașov; a ski resort, high in the mountains above the city. As we followed convoluted hairpins up through the dark forest, we rationalised that we had wanted to check out the ski resort anyway – and there could be puppy-walking opportunities when we got there.

There weren't. And it was hideous. Given the chance to create a resort from scratch, the planners had chosen to construct grotesque tower blocks and huge, characterless hotels that clashed horribly with scenery as pretty as a picture. When he described the UK's National Gallery extension as a 'monstrous carbuncle', Prince Charles coined the perfect phrase to describe the architecture of Poiana Brașov. We drove on.

Approaching Brașov, we dropped straight into a traffic jam. In common with other Romanian cities, parking was not marked on the tourist maps, but signs everywhere promised a tow if you got it wrong. After queueing for nearly thirty minutes at the main round-about, we slowly made our way up Strada George Barițiu. I caught tempting glimpses of an attractive square, pavement restaurants and narrow, medieval streets.

"I think it will be OK when we get parked," I assured Mark. I could see his resolve slipping. Crowds. Tourists. Traffic. Everything that we hate.

There were two spaces remaining in a car park close to the 600-year old Black Church (Biserica Neagră). We gawped at its imposing beauty. Construction had started in 1383, however it got its name when a fire blackened its walls in 1689. Inside and out, bullet holes peppered the walls and in places, bullets were still embedded in the stone; steely mementoes of the revolution and the fall of communism in 1989.

As I looked up to the forested Transylvanian hills that provided a backdrop to the city, a large, white sign announced 'BRASOV' in huge, white 'HOLLYWOOD' letters.

Why?

Fifteen minutes after we had stopped at a table in a pavement café, no-one had served us, so we walked on to the Council Square, Piața Sfatului. By now, I was starving. A sign with pictographs of a dog's head wearing a muzzle and a dog's head struck through with a red line suggested that dogs were not permitted in the square. A full translation of the words eluded us, but we got a sense that dogs were generally not welcome in the whole municipal region of Brașov.

Following a circumnavigation of the square, we entered innocently from a direction whose signs seemed to ban only cartoon bikes and skateboards. I bagged a table at an outdoor restaurant, next to the medieval KFC (Kentucky Fried Chicken), while Mark gave the dogs a drink from a fountain. To my horror, two Romanian policemen made a bee-line towards Mark. He looked like Mrs Honeyman in Camberwick Green, with five dogs milling around his feet. I tensed for a moment, observing their mighty truncheons, then relaxed as they walked straight past. They didn't give Mark and his pack a second glance.

The waiter offered to bring water for the dogs. I didn't court danger by asking whether dogs were permitted in the square. I hoped that Romania's Italian heritage extended beyond disorderly driving to encompass the seemingly innate Latin disregard for rules.

Then. At last. I got bulz.

'A traditional dish of maize polenta, topped with melted cheese and oven-baked in a clay bowl, a well-prepared Transylvanian bulz will keep hunger at bay for a whole day.' All of my previous attempts to try bulz had been thwarted by a trait unique to Romanian restaurants; their unwillingness to serve food.

I got the full Romanian bulz, with bacon, sausage and a fried egg on it. It was decorated with a lovely, little flower, made from shaved beetroot and carrot, folded onto a cocktail stick. I had no doubt that Romanian peasants paid similar attention to presentation.

After eating only half of my bulz, I can promise you that hunger did not trouble the rest of my day.

...

We had a few jobs to do in Brașov. Mark's sandals had now broken, so we waded upstream against tides of tourists to find a sports shop. Irrespective of direction, we were constantly pitted against the tourist tide. Unlike Sighișoara, which oozed atmosphere and smelled of history, the medieval streets of Brașov oozed tourists and smelled of chips.

There were smart shops – but rather like Verona, no walking sandals to be had. I wanted to see Strada Sforii – Rope Street, the narrowest street in Europe, as well as the many medieval Saxon buildings, but I felt like I was drowning in a sea of people.

"I hate it here, shall we just head?" Mark spoke my mind.

Somewhere in its move to modernise, to become

more prosperous and more European, Braşov had lost its charm. We hoped that the same would not happen to the rest of Romania.

Parking cost 15 lei (£3). Foolishly, I started to post a 200 lei note, our smallest remaining denomination, into the parking machine, which promised change. A young Romanian, who happened to be passing, shook his head. I went to buy something in a Magazin Mixt, hoping that they could break such a large note without giving me change in matches. I thought that two cans of Sprite would be a touch miserly, so I added one of their most expensive bottles of Romanian wine to my basket. It still cost only 15 lei, the same as the parking.

A man-sized can of bear spray and a cosh were the other essentials that we picked up from specialist shops on the outskirts. We were now packing rather a lot of what the UK would consider illegal, offensive weapons, although in Romania, for hiking in the wilderness, they were the bear necessities.

'No Dogs' – a sign graced the park in the centre of town. We had considered walking up Tâmpa Hill to tire out the pups, but it was getting late. In any case, we wagered that, being a public space, it too would be 'No Dogs Allowed'.

On our way back to the car park, we had passed a tiny, skeletal old lady dressed in black. Her stretched, waxen face was framed by a headscarf. She backed away from us, retreating into her yard. Raising her hand against the dogs, she had mouthed something, as if uttering an incantation to ward off the evil that is Man's Best Friend.

For us, this summed up Braşov.

35

BRASSED OFF IN BRAȘOV – PART 2

Romania Mania & A Reverse-Engineered Brexit

We overruled Naffsat's judgement to return via the lofty peaks and ski resort and elected to drive back on a straight road through Cristian, which linked Brașov directly to the campsite. It was a great idea for a short cut, until it turned into a 7-mile traffic jam. There was no alternative route, other than joining the traffic jam heading other way – and that led straight back into Brașov.

Brașov exposed us to the zenith of Romania Mania: think Romanian driving, with the addition of mobile phones and the 'far too busy, far too important' attitude of city dwellers.

"I think I'll just close my eyes and not look..." I said as our brakes screeched for the umpteenth time to avoid certain collision.

As we approached the cause of the tailback, it was

clear that someone had not been so careful, or so lucky. The horrifically grim pile-up that we crawled past involved several vehicles and a pedestrian.

Driving through Rașnov, I got a different view of the medieval fortress atop its hill. Clearly the town had no intention of being upstaged by its neighbour, Brașov. Just below the fortress, in case you didn't know or had forgotten, huge, white 'HOLLYWOOD' letters announced 'RASNOV'.

Once again.

Why?

We had originally planned to see eight castles in our seven days in the area. As with Bran, simply driving past Râșnov helped to knock another off the list. Although it looks complete, the fortress is not 'well preserved'. It has been restored in what Hadrian might consider a less than sympathetic way. Like the castle at Bran, a site rich with history has been turned into a tourist trap, filled with acres of kitsch.

However, I did nag Mark until he took a detour through the nearby town of Vulcan.

"It's a good job that you don't do all the trip planning, otherwise, we would only ever go to places with stupid names."

A run-down, one-horse town, Vulcan did not look like a place to 'Live long and prosper'. For the time being, I kept quiet about the Turda salt mines.

...

Back at the campsite, Mark was waved down and taken aside by the nice bloke in the checked shirt. It was obviously a 'chat' – and Mark was gone for some time. Recalling our misdemeanours, my heart, which I had thought was already at rock bottom, sank deeper than a Zen master contemplating deep philosophy from the deepest part of the Kola Superdeep Borehole.

"Have we been evicted?" I asked when he got back.

"Rather the opposite! He has seven dogs and said that dogs should not be on leads, so he's coming with his tractor to move the caravan to a field with no-one around. The dogs can run free – and he even told me not to bother picking up the poo. I said that we're English. We're genetically pre-disposed to pick up poo. And he referred to the Swiss as 'tourists'!"

Lia chortled via email when I told her. "By 'tourists' he means 'amateurs'. He obviously thought that they complained about petty things that are part and parcel of camping. I can just imagine him shaking his head and dismissing them with a wave of his hand!"

Lia was bang on. However, it was an unusual example of an inspired piece of management. Rather than arguing, issuing diktats and creating bad feeling, he had engineered a perfect win-win situation for everyone. We were happy, but were not sure that the Swiss Tourists had it in them to rejoice, even though they had got rid of the Brits in their own, reverse-engineered version of Brexit.

For the first time since we had arrived in this part of Transylvania, my spirits started to lift. Our exile meant that we were alone in an exclusive part of the campsite that was closed to other guests. The dogs could chase around and play joyously. In Splendid Isolation, we opened our expensive bottle of £3 Romanian wine and watched the sun set.

Like a swollen blood corpuscle, suddenly impaled on the sharp, fang-like peaks of the Carpathian Mountains as they blackened into shadow, the brilliant-red solar disc haemorrhaged a sanguine trail that leaked across the livid sky; staining it deep crimson...

That is an exaggeration. It was a pretty sunset, but since we were in pretend-Dracula country, I thought I would deploy a gratuitous blood metaphor.

...

The final sting in the tail of Brașov; Naffsat broke. Fed up with being overruled, it committed suicide, just to spite us. It made a noise like a faulty TV, then subsequently refused to charge. Coincidentally, I had dropped its connector into the dogs' water bowl, but had given it a good shake and left it for a bit. Confident that it had dried out sufficiently to be unrelated to the failure, I could see no reason to mention this to Mark.

So, after all this, it is fair to say: we were Brassed off in Brașov.

36

PREJMER FORTRESS & PELEȘ CASTLE

Ramparts, Royalty & Saxon Big Brother

Afore we beat our hasty retreat from the touristic trav-
esties of Bran and Brașov, I must tell you about Prejmer
and Peleș, which are not to be missed. Mark and I
agreed that Prejmer was one of the best things that we
have ever experienced.

UNESCO-listed Prejmer Citadel is the largest forti-
fied church in South Eastern Europe and among the
most important medieval monuments in Transylvania.
It was built in 1212 by Teutonic Knights, donated to the
Cistercians from Cârța and was later taken on by local
Saxons.

Sitting at the eastern extremity of Transylvania,
close to the Buzău Pass, Prejmer was right on the front
line of attack – and it means business. Strengthened
and expanded in several phases over the centuries, it
finally became the obstinate, unyielding, white mono-

lith that sits belligerently in the landscape today. All I can say to the Tatars, Turks, Mongols or anyone else with designs on forcing Prejmer's submission is "Good luck with that!"

The defences are impressive. The moated, circular walls are 40ft high and 16ft thick, with towers, bulwarks, iron gates and drawbridges. Prejmer's ingenious 'Death Organ' is not to be found inside the church; it was a spinning board with an array of five guns on each side. Each set of five could be fired simultaneously, while the other five were being recharged. Continuous fire delivered by this ingenious weapon could wreak devastating damage to the enemy.

In its 500 years on the front line, Prejmer was besieged fifty times, but captured only once, when the defenders ran out of drinking water. This is all the more impressive when you consider that Prejmer was a peasant fortress, not a military one.

Prejmer's purpose was to allow village life to continue as normally as possible when the community was under attack. Inside are 272 rooms, built into the whitewashed, defensive walls like cells in a beehive. In a disorderly arrangement over four floors, the rooms are accessed by doors in the inner wall, making it look like a crazy advent calendar. Access to the doors is via an uneven, rickety network of dark, wooden walkways and ladders.

There was a room for each family. The door numbers correlated with their house numbers in the village and apparently, locals still retain the right to use their allocated rooms. Inside the fortress was a well, a bakery and a school. Thus, the mild inconvenience of being besieged by a ravening horde provided no excuse for bunking off lessons. Underground passages facilitated the storage and transport of food.

It was charming to find that preparations for times of war went beyond the physical aspects of defence and supplies. How would you get on, spending indeterminate periods of time incarcerated with your nearest and dearest, along with all the neighbours? Prejmer was the Saxon version of the 'Big Brother' house. I loved the legend of the 'Chamber of Reconciliation'. An early form of marriage guidance, a couple who argued would be locked in a room with only one bowl. They were forced to stay there and share until they sorted out their differences. There was plenty of incentive; in this version of Big Brother, eviction meant taking your chances with a host of rapacious Turks.

I smiled to think that Mark and I spend most of our time in a Chamber of Reconciliation; it's called a caravan. At least Saxon couples just had to live together during times of war. They were spared the stress of co-operating over an awning. (It is well known that erecting an awning: the independently-minded 'tent' on the side of a caravan, is a feat of complexity equivalent to the moon landing – and well-recognised as a catalyst for divorce.)

The entrance to the fortress passed through a 100ft-long, arched tunnel. It opened into the Baker's Court, which was separate from the rest of the fortress; probably as a fire precaution. Blade didn't manage to join the Puppy Pose in front of the massive, protective oak and iron portcullis. Mark and I took turns to Fur Babysit in the peaceful, inner gardens as we spent several hours exploring the maze of wooden walkways.

Some of the rooms were open to visitors and we investigated the dank, stone passageway that followed the full, inner circumference of the defensive walls. Looking out through the loopholes from the spooky, dim interior brought to life how it must have felt to be trapped inside, surrounded by screaming enemies, intent on your demise. We could almost fantasise that we were in Castle Black in 'Game of Thrones', defending the Seven Kingdoms from the horrors of the North.

We left Prejmer with a real feeling that we had made contact with history.

...

Parked up in the scenic town of Sinaia, a winter ski resort, we went in search of its many twos and firsts. First up, two castles for the price of one; Peleș and Pelișor, the Little and Large of the castle world. Peleș was founded in 1873 as a summer palace for Romania's first King, a German-born chap called Carol I, who presided over a period of peace and prosperity in Romania. Finished in 1883, Peleș is a 'Neo-Renaissance' castle, although an educated, architectural expert like myself would refer to it as 'Disney-Styley'.

Pelișor, the 'Art Nouveau' castle next door, was founded by Ferdinand, Carol's successor. In castle architecture terms, this is 'Not Disney-Styley'. Ferdi obviously felt that a modest 70 rooms, furnished with Lalique and Tiffany, was more homely and less showy-offy than 160 themed rooms, filled with priceless artworks, frescoes, Murano crystal, Cordoba leather-covered walls or handmade silk tapestries on the ceiling.

Besides being one of the most striking castles in Europe, Peleș was the first to be lit entirely by electricity, provided by its own, hydroelectric plant. It was also the first place in Romania to screen a movie.

Apparently Ceaușescu had his eye on it, but its caretakers saved it by telling him that it was inhabited by a deadly fungus.

Many trendy cafés were dotted along Sinaia's streets, so we started our visit fortified by coffee. Rows of spooky and imposing gothic buildings suggested that Sinaia might at one time have been home to the families Munster and Adams.

A cobbled, tree-lined footpath climbed from the town to the castle past Sinaia Monastery. The monastery, one of Romania's oldest, was founded in 1695 by Prince Mihail Cantacuzino, following his pilgrimage to Egypt to visit the real Mount Sinai (where Moses received the Ten Commandments). Unsurprisingly, dogs were not permitted in the monastery, museum and its two churches (the 'Old' and the 'New') so we admired it in passing as we continued up to the castle.

Stalls selling Romanian handicrafts and tourist trinkets lined our route, although this did not detract from our first sight of the fantasy castle, with its delicate, needle-like towers. It sat in a bucolic backdrop of green, with Alpine peaks rising in the distance. It was clear why this landscape had captivated King Carol.

It was Monday; the castle was closed; visits were by guided tour only and, undoubtedly, dogs would not have been allowed inside. Nevertheless, it was a pleasure to wander in the sunshine and admire the stunning exterior and the gardens. Although the crowds were sparse, the pups attracted plenty of attention, particularly when they took it upon themselves to pile into a fountain for a cooling dip before we had a chance to get them back on their leads. Although Bladeless, a perfectly lined-up Puppy Pose on the steps in front of the castle has probably now gone viral.

The positive of being in a tourist destination was cake. We took five at a shady table, overlooking fields and the castle, watching a man scythe hay. A guitarist serenaded us outside the café. He loved the dogs and took a picture on his mobile to send to his brother in London.

At Peleş, we had our first encounter with a pack of five or six small but aggressive strays, led by a bull terrier with a scarred face and no ears. Having Blade batting for our team was like having Crocodile Dundee as your guide in the Australian Outback. Blade is not a large dog, but he has presence. A slight raise of the wolf-like ruff on his hackles as he maintained a confident trot was all that our Street Kid needed to do to assert protective rights over his new family. The strays kept a respectful distance.

Back at the campsite, we enjoyed our last Southern Transylvanian sunset in our field. The following day, Kismet would strike north.

37

CAMPSITE VARALJA, GHEORGHENI

Lacul Roşu & The Bicaz Gorge – Driving Into 'The Neck of Hell'

'Water, water everywhere, nor any drop to drink.'

Our arrival at Campsite Varalja, just on the outskirts of Gheorgheni, was a little more dramatic than we'd hoped. With much coaxing, Naffsat had taken on sufficient charge to guide us for the final two minutes of our approach to the campsite. Then, literally as we turned into the drive, Blade vomited.

The site was heavenly; a tranquil, floral haven of green lawn and shady trees. The only downside was the water. The campsite had its own well, which was nearly dry. We filled up our Aquaroll with what looked like a cup of tea made from nothing but Gilberts. It clogged the pump – making a supermarket run for bottled water our top priority. Unfortunately, addressing Blade's laundry looked out of the question.

My friend Tim had worked in Tomsk. He poo-pooed our horror, telling us, "I spent three years bathing, drinking and washing up in water like that."

I have told you before that buying maps abroad is a tricky business. There are eighteen marked walking trails in the Bicaz Gorge alone – and the gorge was part of a larger national park. During his supermarket run, Mark popped into the local Tourist Information.

"Do you have any maps?"

"No."

Half-way out of the door, Mark was treated to a barely relevant afterthought:

"There's a map shop around the corner."

In the map shop, they had maps of everywhere, except the local area.

"We have a map of Lacul Roșu (Red Lake)."

"But I want to walk around here – there are lots of beautiful walks around Gheorgheni."

"Everybody goes to Lacul Roșu to walk."

Subject closed.

In Romania, electronics were expensive. Replacing Naffsat seemed unlikely, although Mark averted Blade's laundry crisis by purchasing a shipping load of extra, red fleece blankets in the sale at Kaufland.

Relaxing in the sun, the smell of wood smoke wafted over from a group of friendly Hungarians who were having B&B (Barbecue and Beer.) It was 'Take the Kids to Work' day in the field next door. A mare with foal at foot was pulling a strange contraption, which turned the hay to dry. It had four thin, wooden legs, which kicked out to the rear. They threw hay up into the air while beating a rhythm like a Duracell Bunny playing the drums. It provided a surprisingly relaxing audio scape to our whole stay.

...

"'Lie Down' is a very powerful psychological position of surrender and acceptance and 'Roll Over' shows that he means no harm and is confident enough to be vulnerable."

To help him in his new life, my friend Nicky of 'Chilled Out Dogs' dispensed training advice for Blade. About ten minutes later, she followed up with,

"Let me know when he has mastered that – and message me if you need some tips to help him learn."

I thought that it might take Blade a couple of days to get there. I was dewy-eyed as I sent Nicky a photo of Blade rolling over before I even received her second email. He grasped the whole drill in fewer than five minutes. We were in no doubt; Bladey Boy is a most amazing dog.

...

With no map, we followed 'everybody' and walked at Lacul Roşu, the largest mountain lake in Romania. The lake was formed when a beautiful, green-eyed girl called Eszter was kidnapped and held prisoner in a cave. She wept and called upon the mountain to help her. Muntele Ucigaș, the Killer Mount, took pity on her and pledged to solve her plight. As good as its word, it flattened her under a landslide, along with her kidnapper and possibly a shepherd and his sheep. Killer Mounts are like that. Reputedly, the lake is red from their blood.

A more unlikely explanation connects the formation of the lake with an earthquake in 1838. This precipitated a landslip, which formed a natural dam. In the sun, red stone, coloured by iron oxides (rust), is reflected in the lake. Iron-bearing soils also wash into the lake from the Red Stream (and into our well in Gheorgheni). Tree tops poking out of the water, the remains of a flooded forest, lend some credibility to this story, although personally, I think it's a load of fanciful rubbish. I know this because I gazed into the mysterious waters and was greeted by the fabled green of Eszter's eyes.

At 3,225ft, the temperature was perfect for walking. We followed a well-trodden path around the lake and were joined by a delightful, disabled puppy. He had a withered back leg; we could see no sign of trauma, so perhaps he had just been born with defective ligaments. (Otherwise, he would have been coming with us to the vet!) He followed us for the full circumnavigation and enjoyed playing with The Famous Five. His disability didn't seem to slow him down and due to his sweet nature, we had to have another stern chat with ourselves.

The view across the lake to the limestone mountains was outstandingly pretty, but the village itself was a tourist trap. Thankfully, we had managed to arrive before the main wave of coaches. At least this meant that we didn't have to go hungry. There was a wide choice of restaurants; we filled up on goulash in one, before watching our chimney cake being hand made on a stall overlooking the lake. Then, we found the puppy again and treated him to a tin of beef and salmon before we left.

We carried on to the Bicaz Gorge, a narrow canyon. which wiggles through the Eastern Carpathians, joining Transylvania with Moldova. It was our third 'Dangerous Road', after the Transalpina and Trans-făgărășan.

Part of the Cheile Bicazului-Hășmaș National Park, Bicaz is one of the main rock-climbing areas in Romania. It boasts the greatest number of maximum-difficulty routes and the odd Via Ferrata. As the road nipped and tucked around 1,000ft Jurassic limestone walls, we were confronted with a monumental, white obelisk; the Oltarko – 'Altar Rock'. Towering 3,793ft high, with a crucifix on its summit, it was first climbed in the 1930s. It stood as a guardian; as we passed, we entered the 'Neck of Hell', Gâtul Iadului, where the gorge narrowed and huge, overhanging rocks blotted out the sky.

Lacking a proper map, we were unable to find the entrance to the 12.5-mile Bicajel Valley, where we had hoped to hike. Hidden behind the high walls, it promised caves, waterfalls, alpine plains and small traditional villages – and possibly bears, wolves and lynx. Many pedestrians walked the gorge on a pathway next to the road, but with the traffic, stalls and craft bazaars dotted along the route, that held no appeal to us.

Despite the draw of walks through the Snowdrop cave with its stalactites, The Fairies' Garden and the Black and Waterfall caves, we had to move on from Gheorgheni. We couldn't cope with the well. Dishes had to be rinsed with spring water, the laundry situation was well out of hand and I had been forced into wet-wipe-washes; something I thought that I had abandoned along with my youth at Glastonbury in the '90s.

To this day, our pump and Aquaroll are stained from Gheorgheni's water. It won't stop us from coming back, though. Once we have bought some maps.

38

GHEORGHENI TO SUCEVIȚA – CAMP CRISTAL

U-Turn If U Want To & Our Second Cornfield Crossing

"That's a country road. It's how all country roads should be, not tarmacked like in Britain. You're in the country, not in the middle of town. Pfffft!"

"F'in tourists" – I think that was Lia's inference when we commented on the state of the roads.

Still, it was a route of 1000 perfect views. As we twisted up into the Eastern Carpathians, altitude intensified the spread of autumn's bronze mosaic. Tree-tops burned a little redder and orchards bent under the weight of apples, like a crop of shiny cricket balls. Piles of orange pumpkins were massed against white-washed walls. The architecture changed; wooden homes with shingle roofs, edged with ornate filigree-work, looked like Victorian cricket pavilions. The sky burned blue, with artful wisps of white cloud daubed tastefully above the ever-changing vistas.

It was still 30°C. Subtle, autumnal aromas drifted in through Big Blue's windows; wood smoke; burning leaves; heady and herbal scents, like honeysuckle or thyme; the sweet smell of hay and newly cut wood. There was activity everywhere. The countryside was alive with shepherds tending flocks, people hand-picking maize and potatoes, scything the verges for fodder or turning the last of the hay by hand.

The views across the mountains were stupendous; they crept into the distance like a restless ocean of forested waves, rising and falling as far as the eye could see. Battalions of hay ricks populated the fields; wide, solid ones like small bungalows or thinner ones that looked like dried-up cypress trees or Chewbacca mustering his own army of giant wookies.

Naffsat-less, we had to resort to map-reading. It was so baffling that I wished that I had also had a compass.

Everything went smoothly until we encountered a confusing junction. We missed the turn onto Mark's proposed route, although that wasn't a huge problem. It left us on the route that I had planned, which followed the more major roads through Suceava. Mark had wanted to avoid the town, since we were towing a large caravan, but I wasn't worried. The map showed a substantial ring road, the 2P, running around the outskirts.

Well, who knows where the 2P is? Having driven there, I certainly don't. It didn't seem to exist. The road layout bore no correlation to the map and, to add to the interest, there were no road signs. I imagined the justification, "Who needs signs? Everyone knows the way!"

We took a wrong turn. I maintained that we should have gone straight on, even though it did look like it led into a housing estate, but Mark hung a hasty left. At least the wrong turn oriented me to where we were on the map.

"We definitely should have taken that road!"

We drove miles into the countryside before we found space to execute a U-Turn; never simple for a caravan on a small, country road. Back at the same junction, I had to concur that the housing estate option looked dodgy, so we tried straight on. At some traffic lights, Mark leaned out of the van window to ask directions from the car next door.

"Do you speak English? Which road is this? Does it lead to Sucevița? There are no signs!"

With a shrug, the driver acknowledged all points, but confirmed that we were on the right road.

Having almost bypassed Suceava and resolved never to come back, UNESCO World Heritage status or no, our tribulations were not over. The left turn for Rădăuți was another befuddling junction.

"Why is Rădăuți signed straight on and not left?"

I soon found out. The road was closed and a diversion in place, so the caravan was treated to its second cornfield crossing. We shared our field with HGVs and horse carts, perplexed as to why we were the ones getting funny looks. There was no sign at the end of the field. An HGV crossed the road and continued through the fields.

"I am sure that it's left onto this road..." My map-reading confidence was shaken. "If we come to Satu Mare in a minute, we're on the right road..."

Thankfully, Satu Mare hove into view. But Rădăuți was another major junction point which saw no purpose in providing signs. We went the wrong way and executed another complicated U-Turn on a tree-lined boulevard. Final verification that we were on the road to Sucevița came from a sign placed conveniently 100-yards after the junction.

Thankfully, Blade had not been sick, despite seven hours in the car, bumpy wrong turns and the cornfield. It was such a relief to arrive at Camp Cristal. Without Naffsat, homing in on well-concealed campsites took skill. Operating my iPhone and laptop simultaneously from Mission Control (the passenger seat) as we edged our way up the main road through Sucevița, I looked like Rick Wakeman manning banks of keyboards at a Prog Rock concert. While my keyboard skills might not have re-created Wakeman's 'Journey to the Centre of the Earth', I did score a hole-in-one on Camp Cristal's entrance.

As Mark pitched, I walked the dogs up the banks of the Sucevița River, which was directly adjacent to the campsite. The width of the river bed suggested that in spate, it was a furious torrent, although the summer level was little more than a trickle. There were temporary foot bridges, made of rope and planks, as well as fords for vehicles and horses. The pooches had a great time. Three of them managed to roll in a towering pile of horse poo, while the other two simply achieved the full mud-crust. Thankfully, we had clean water rather than gritty tea on tap, right next to our pitch: a small luxury – like a smooth, metalled road – that you take completely for granted until you have had to go for three days without washing properly or tow your caravan through a field.

The moon rose like a luminous candy floss, blurred around the edges by pale pink wisps of cloud. After rinsing the dogs, we cracked open a couple of well-deserved cold ones and snuggled up with five tired, but acceptably cleansed and fragrant puppies.

39

SUCEVIȚA & MOLDOVIȚA

Action, Adventure & Painted Monasteries

Mânăstirea Sucevița, Sucevița's Painted Monastery, is an Eastern Orthodox convent. It was just up the road, UNESCO-listed – and it was a real wow.

The twenty-two painted monasteries of Bukovina are absolute treasures; covered both inside and out with rich and vibrant Byzantine murals. Stephen the Great, ruler and saint, started the trend among Moldavian princes of founding a monastery each time he won a battle.

The paintings were exquisite; true masterpieces. They date from the 15th and 16th Centuries, when most people were illiterate. The frescoes portray stories from the Bible in a way that the peasants could understand. Delightfully, the buildings and paintings have changed little over the centuries.

Just walking through the gates at Sucevița was

breathtaking. The shimmering gold and jewel hues of the exterior frescoes sang in the sunshine. Viewing it from the colourful gardens, surrounded by high, defensive walls, it was a meditative, peaceful space. The only nod to commercialism was a large, blue plastic barrel with a tap, labelled 'Holy Water'. Don't forget to bring a bottle!

Each painted monastery has its own distinctive colour and, 500 years on, the formula for the pigments remains a mystery. Sucevița is blue-green. Founded in 1581, Sucevița was the last, largest and finest of the twenty-two to be built. Legend has it that work stopped when a painter fell to his death and that is why the western exterior was left un-decorated. Despite this, Sucevița still boasts the greatest number of images. Its signature fresco is the 'Ladder of Virtues', where red-winged angels escort the righteous to heaven, while sinners fall through the rungs into the eternal torment of grinning devils.

Obviously, dogs were not allowed and as a gesture of respect, I was asked to wear a skirt over my shorts. I had taken a sarong for just such an eventuality but as I paid my entrance fee, the nun indicated a row of hooks.

"You can pick up a skirt on the left." It reminded me of the crucifixion scene in Monty Python's *Life of Brian*, when Brian and his fellows were lined up on the left and instructed to collect one cross each.

Mark and I took turns to sit with the dogs outside. A pretty, young stray took a shine to Blade. It was extremely mutual. I had to tell him sternly that he couldn't have sex on a Sunday, especially outside a House of God, although that did not stop him from trying quite hard. She was a sweet, gentle little girl; black and beige with pale, quizzical eyebrows and a wonderfully soft coat. They played together for ages. It was a mistake on my part to give her a name; Buffy (another Vampire Slayer). But really. We couldn't...

We drove on to Moldovița on the 17A, 'the most scenic road in Romania'. The views at the top of the pass were inspiring, so we stopped for lunch and a walk. Bukovina – 'the land of the beeches' is characterised by its 'Obcine' – parallel rows of hills, which sported skirts of their own. Their modesty was preserved by forests of beech and conifer.

...

At Moldovița, a kind-faced young nun dressed in black greeted us at the door. She asked about the dogs. I told her about Kai and Rosie's work as therapy dogs in a Care Home.

"Animals really enrich people's lives," she agreed. But they still weren't allowed in.

I donned my skirt again. The monastery was another utterly magical place. Predominantly gold and blue, Moldovița's signature frescoes are the 'Tree of Jesse '– Christ's family tree and the 'Siege of Constantinople', a fine example of political spin from the 1500s. The mural cunningly substitutes the Persians, who *did* attack the Byzantine capital in 626, with the contemporary enemy of the people, the Turks.

At least no-one had painted the 8th Commandment next to it. 'Thou shalt not bear false witness against thy neighbour.'

We drove on to Voronet, 'The Sistine Chapel of the East', painted in such rich shades of blue on blue that it has its own designation 'Voronet Blue'. It was now nearly 5pm and we hit a traffic jam in Gura Humorului. As we approached, we noted a large tailback on the road joining from Voronet. The risk was finding the monastery closed, then having to queue for hours to get back to where we started, so we left it for next time.

With hindsight, this was a good decision. Little did we suspect that our trip back would be quite so interesting – or so long. We saw the funny side; we were following the River Humor after all. The road No177 that was clearly marked on the map became a dirt track about three-quarters of the way back to Sucevița. Then, it petered out in a forest.

We had no option but to retrace our route for miles. A hasty swerve into a difficult-to-spot cut-off to Pleșa put us on the 209L. Since it had a number and everything – and seemed to pass through several villages – we were confident that the 209L was a safe option. How little we had learned about Romanian roads. It was basically a rocky track, rather like a river bed, that rose up a 10 per cent gradient to a hilltop church. Here, Mark and I had a navigational disagreement.

"I saw a sign to Sucevița"

"It's a footpath..." I clarified.

Although we stuck to the road, the van slalomed down through a forest on a surface of slippery mud. It did get us back, although our 50-mile return journey took over two hours – and we really did see the cows come home. Romanian cows know where they live; once the field gate is opened, they go home on their own!

It had been a perfect day, though. Tired doggies after their blast around the hills; jaw-dropping sights, both natural and man-made – and on the way back, we drove through a town with a rude name.

Let's just say that it begins with 'C', rhymes with 'Flit' – and I am surprised that any men can find it.

40

SUCEVIȚA TO BREB – THE TRAUMATIC 24

Desperately Seeking Breb

Neither of us said anything, but we were both looking out for someone as we towed the caravan past the monastery in Sucevița,

"Buffy's not there…" I spoke for both of us.

Buffy was there, further on. We pulled over and had the sternest talk yet with ourselves. Travelling with six dogs was not possible. It might stall us at our first border, never mind when we attempted to enter the UK. We continued tearfully, consoling ourselves that she lived in a year-round, working village. We had seen that people left out food for the stray dogs. She would be OK…

We re-traced our steps to Moldovița Monastery on the DN17. Continuing over the Muntii Rodnei National Park, we saw snippets of a 31-mile mountain ridge, among the longest in Romania. Since we had made such good time, we opted to miss out our interim campsite and push on to Breb in Maramureș, our final stop in Romania.

Then we hit the DN18. Blade was improving in the van, but the unmade road proved too much and he vomited. The road state presented additional concerns; 100 miles to go and no campsites en route. At this pace, we would never make it. Thankfully, we hit macadam at Ciocănești, nine miles later, but as we climbed, we encountered snow, which we had not expected in September.

Two weeks previously, with temperatures in the mid-30°s, it had frequently been too hot to go outside. Snow had already closed the Transfăgărășan, so on reaching Prislop Monastery at 4,793ft, perhaps we should not have been surprised. Taking photos of the wintry landscape wearing shorts was a chilly business, especially when, concentrating on the view, my sandaled foot broke through ice and entered a freezing puddle.

It was reassuring to know that we had snow chains and winter tyres; it was just a shame that they were in our garage, back in the UK.

Approaching Breb, the vista before us was the most beautiful that we have ever seen; fertile fields framed by mountain ridges, whose crags and natural highlights were rosy and gilded by the setting sun. Some-where near Ocna Șugatag, I knew that we had passed the turning on the map for Breb, but there had been no road signs. I had spotted a small, dirt road; that couldn't have been it. Surely.

Once again, I invoked the aid of the laptop for more accurate directions to reach the village. I was convinced that Breb was nearby, but the roads on the screen were too faint to see. It was beginning to get dark; we were in the middle of nowhere, seeking a place that didn't seem to exist. The road appeared to be leading us inexorably into a mountainous wilderness and there was nowhere to turn our mighty length around. I could feel the first, slight tingle of unease beginning to set in.

We thought that we must have already missed Breb by miles, when we finally saw a sign. Turning almost back on ourselves to take the narrow road, we passed beneath the village's magnificent, carved portal; a pillared, wooden gate, so typical of Maramureş. We had found Breb. Now we needed to find the campsite.

The sun was balanced atop the indigo Carpathian peaks. Fragrant smoke from autumnal fires drifted over shadowy regiments of hay ricks in the fields. As we meandered down into the village centre with our large caravan, a small gathering guessed our purpose. They shouted and pointed.

"Camping. That way!"

We bounced up an unmade road and I could have cried with joy when we finally found the campsite. It was just twilight. We were saved! After that, everything went perfectly to plan.

Of course it didn't. This was the Traumatic 24 and

we were only nine hours in. We are The Ca-Lamberti on tour; it was never going to be straightforward.

We couldn't get into the campsite. The owner came to help, but there wasn't enough room to manoeuvre. The road was narrow, as was the 90-degree turn into the site, which was also up a steep slope. As we swung in, Caravan Kismet's nearside wheel stuck fast on a set of steps to the left of the rise. We jiggled about but after several attempts, during which the back grounded out, we accepted that we could not align ourselves to turn without catching the steps. With Kismet unhitched, we tried to pull her into a better position by hand. We were tired; we had been lost; we had been driving for nine hours on tricky mountain roads; the caravan was blocking the road and by now, it was pitch dark.

With impeccable timing, the bolt that holds the jockey wheel on to the front of the caravan sheared.

With no jockey wheel to support her nose, Kismet became a giant see saw.

...

There have been few such moments on our travels: times when clearly the best course of action is to collapse to the ground, cradle your head in your hands, rock backwards and forwards and weep uncontrollably.

We couldn't do that, because we had to use all our strength to hold up the nose of a 1.5T caravan, try to man-handle it into a position where we could re-hitch and then complete a seemingly impossible manoeuvre to ensure that we were no longer blocking the road – and, as a bonus, had a bed for the night.

I started directing traffic, including a horse and cart; the campsite owner supported Kismet's nose as Mark hauled her out of the way. With some super-human team efforts, we managed to re-hitch. Then, our non-English-speaking host shared two precious nuggets of information. The first:

"*Parlo Italiano*." He spoke Italian.

The second: "*Duecento metri – girare.*"

200m further along the narrow road, we could turn around to enter from the other direction, taking advantage of both a shallower incline and a shallower turn.

Now that we had grounded out the back of the caravan and annihilated our jockey wheel, we thanked him profusely for his timely advice.

Finally on site, we left Kismet hitched, with Big Blue fulfilling the role of acting jockey wheel. Typically, the pitch was anything but level front to back but we had no option but to live with it. At least we now know that you can sleep on a steep incline if you face uphill.

It took half an hour to fill our 40L Aquaroll from the trickle of a tap in the owner's house. I thought that he might think that I had moved in permanently if I filled the toilet flush tank as well, so I improvised. You never stop learning; I can tell you now that a caravan flush pump and a bottle of fizzy water is not a match made in heaven.

Electricity arrived in the form of a substantial, rolled-up cable – a well-attested fire hazard. I connected up, but made sure that I placed the roll somewhere in the deep blackness, well away from the caravan.

With Big Blue and Kismet inextricably conjoined, popping to the shops was out of the question. Thankfully, we had picked up some supplies en route, although we could only muster the energy to make a ham sandwich. We cracked open a bottle of warm Weissbier. It was the best that we'd ever tasted.

The climate had definitely cooled. Outside, directing traffic and solving issues with the caravan, I had been able to see my breath. Inside, Kismet was freezing. We retreated under blankets and put on *Bridget Jones's Diary*. We were in the midst of a catastrophe, thousands of miles from home and it was the first time that we had felt homesick. Somehow, the romantic tribulations of a thirtysomething in the familiar predictability of London and the Home Counties was the salve that our souls needed.

However, there was still a nagging doubt in our minds. The site bore no resemblance to the photos that we had seen on the web and we appeared to be camped in somebody's garden.

41

BREB TO BREB – "WE BOLDLY GO WHERE NO VAN HAS GONE BEFORE"

Never Mind the Cornfield... The Rocky Road to Babou Maramures

By morning, we were certain that we were in the wrong campsite. Despite the owner's kindness, we needed to move on. We were in his garden, not level and had to set up a shorthold tenancy each time we wanted water.

Further web research revealed that we were less than half a mile from our target, Camping Babou Maramures. The garden was too small for us to turn around, forcing us to reverse out the way we had come. Kismet grounded out again for old time's sake and emerged facing away from our destination.

"Should we walk the dogs to Babou and scope out the route?"

Mark was not keen. He set off in 'piece of cake' mode with Kismet in tow. Breb village centre opened out into a little square.

"We could turn around here..." I suggested.

"Nah. How bad can it be?"

Mark's famous last words. Two months on Romanian roads. Had he learned nothing?

...

Soon, the whole of Breb knew that The English had arrived. We had drawn ourselves a rudimentary map of how to approach Babou Maramures from the opposite direction to the short and sensible 0.5-mile route along the 'main' village road. However, Breb is a picturesque labyrinth of small, dirt roads, many too small to be featured in our atlas or even on Google maps. Thus, the route that we had sketched bore no resemblance to the reality of Breb.

We attracted some funny looks as we evaded obstacles, such as a horse-drawn hay cart on a road that was wide enough for only one vehicle. Most Breb residents still use horse-power – substituting their carts for sleighs in the winter. A few people who we asked along the way confirmed that our route led to Babou, so we forged on.

I mean, how bad could it be?

It started off moderately bad. Of course, like Patsy and Rod, who had told us about driving their motorhome over a mountain, once committed to steep, narrow, unmade roads with a long vehicle, there is no going back.

Then, it got worse. It narrowed so much that I had

to get out and walk ahead of the caravan, carefully checking clearances to the front, back and sides as we made painfully slow progress.

An exasperated man rushed out of his house. This proved helpful; we needed him to move his car to facilitate our 90-degree turn back on to the 'main' village road. As we emerged from the junction, he touched the side of his head in a gesture that suggested 'You have a screw loose!'

"*This* is the road" he roared, waving expansively up and down the street. He stabbed an accusing finger towards Kismet and spluttered "*That* is a footpath!"

The footpath which the caravan had just negotiated was shown clearly in our atlas as one of only two main roads that entered the village. Footpath status explained last night's absence of a road sign. We praised our good fortune that we had missed it; otherwise, we would have been forced to haplessly cope with its vicissitudes in the impenetrable darkness of the remote countryside.

Ah well, we had made it. Except that we hadn't yet. I didn't know whether to laugh or cry when I saw the approach road to Babou Maramures. Another narrow, 90-degree bend up what looked like the rocky bed of a dry, mountain stream.

Evelyn, the Dutch campsite owner, stared in awe at Big Blue and Kismet as I checked in.

"That's the biggest vehicle we've ever had! How did you get around that last corner? On our website, we stipulate 'no caravans longer than 5m'."

We hadn't studied the website. Kismet is 7.2m, towed by a 5m van. Nearly the length of an articulated lorry.

"Is your van 4-wheel drive?" asked Matthias, Evelyn's husband.

"Er, no…"

His face said it all. "You've done really well…"

Like Patsy and Rod, we had, at last, truly earned our colours as Adventure Caravanners:

'To boldly go where no van has gone before.'

...

Having completed the heroics, our task was simple; pitch and level, without the luxury of a jockey wheel. It took some time; a lot of jiggling about; some unsuccessful bodging with duct tape and the use of our gripper tracks. Our lack of 4-wheel drive was very evident as we slid around on the site's grassy slopes. Finally, with Kismet's front shored up with a log of perfect dimensions, scavenged from Matthias' wood pile, we realised that we were in paradise.

Yesterday, we had identified the most beautiful place in Romania; wherever you are at the time. Now, we changed our minds. Breb is the most beautiful place in Romania, if not the world.

'The Village Under the Mountain' sits beneath the Creasta Cocoşului – the edge of an ancient volcanic crater, eroded into the shape of a cock's comb. Breb rests in a sheltered bowl, like a little Garden of Eden, frozen in time.

Finally relaxing in the sunshine with Mark and the dogs, I felt as happy as I have ever been. I could smell woodsmoke and see people toiling in the fields, close to nature.

A flock of goldfinches flitted in the long grass.

42

UNESCO STAVE CHURCHES – BÂRSANA, IEUD, POIENILE IZEI & GLOD

The Wooden Wonders of Maramureş

It was a stunning, golden September morning, with the moon still hanging lazily in the sky as the sun came up. It was a cool start, but sunshine soon warmed the air.

We drove out the way that we should have come, via the main road through Breb. It differed in one major way from the footpath; it was slightly wider.

Everywhere we looked, there was activity – people in traditional dress were collecting apples or raking hay. We realised that what made the Romanian countryside so beautiful was that it was lived in and loved. The locals worked the land by hand. This was no dead landscape of mechanised monoculture, filled with deserted villages like so much of Europe. Life took place outside. Everywhere we went, old ladies in black sat in rows, chatting and watching the world go by;

men gathered to enjoy a convivial beer; mothers and grandmothers laughed and played with children while ducks and chickens ran around the hedgerows.

The plan was to visit some of the wooden stave churches for which Maramureș is famed. Hundreds were constructed between the 1500s and 1700s, when the Austro-Hungarian Catholic nobles banned Orthodox Romanians from building stone churches.

Thankfully, Maramureș already had a long tradition of timber architecture to counter this religious persecution. We saw Maramureș wooden gates everywhere. These elaborately carved, three-pillared wooden portals date back to feudal times and have a spiritual role in protecting the inhabitants. They grace the entrances of villages, churches and houses and bear symbols such as the sun, the tree of life, ropes, snakes and the wolf's tooth.

Miraculously, these outstanding carpentry skills are still nurtured in this remarkable county. Maramureș is a living, breathing museum of medieval, village culture. Today, around one hundred stave churches remain, of which eight are UNESCO listed.

We struggled to find the first, in Bârsana. We found a wooden church, craftsmen carving wood, a stray dog who followed us and an Italian windsurfer, curious to know where we windsurfed in Romania.

"Torbole, Lago di Garda. On the way back."

He approved of our Italian RRD boards. "The same as mine!"

Eventually, we discovered the real stave church on

top of the hill. It was stunningly pretty; small, with a thin, needle-like steeple; the patina of the weathered wood shone in the sun. The setting was arresting; the Creasta was clearly visible and at last, we could place Breb within the landscape.

We had been in two minds about stopping at the monastery in Bârsana – until we saw a hint of its grandeur from the road. Although it is modern, completed in 1997 on the site of an older structure, it is a strikingly beautiful complex of wooden buildings, re-created in traditional Maramureş style. It was inspiring to see that such skill and craftsmanship could still exist. The new, shingle roofs were captivating – still un-weathered and golden, they seemed to flow around the buildings in liquid curves. Until the completion of the new monastery, the 187ft steeple of Bârsana's original stave church had made it the tallest wooden building in Europe.

No-one seemed to mind the dogs joining us in the grounds. They are God's creatures, after all. Blade finally nailed the Puppy Pose in the colourful gardens, sitting sedately in formation with the Fab Four in front of the dazzling architecture.

Sightseeing starvation was averted by a number of snack stalls located in the car park. Even those were beautiful, copying the style of the other monastery buildings. In the shade, next to a tinkling waterfall, I tried a cabbage bread, Mark a cheese one, with pumpkin doughnuts for afters.

'The Church on the Hill' at Ieud was my favourite

of the stave churches. UNESCO listed, Ieud is the oldest wooden church in Romania; built in 1364 and dedicated to 'The Birth of the Mother of God'. We took turns to view the beautifully painted interior, which was agreeably cool, compared to the warmth outside. The graveyard was very moving; most tombstones bore pictures of the deceased. It seemed much more personal than a standard inscription of 'beloved mum/dad/sister/brother of...' (delete as appropriate).

From the top of the churchyard, I gazed out and photographed the countryside. Spires of several other stave churches nestled amid the verdant landscape. A man waved and beckoned from the church, so I wandered back. Signs everywhere dictated 'no photos' to protect the colourful, painted interior, but he encouraged me to take photos without flash. I sent Mark back in to add a further contribution to the collection box, since the curator had been so kind. As we were leaving, the man offered me a small bottle of floral scent to sniff. When I said that I liked it, he indicated that it was for me. A small thing, but just so wonderfully typical of the generosity that we had experienced everywhere in Romania.

We drove back via Poienile Izei and Glod. Poienile Izei was my least favourite stave church; another UNESCO World Heritage Site, it could not have been a more contrasting experience. Mark hadn't even got out of the van when the keyholder ran over to yell at me in French; dogs were "*Interdit!* – Forbidden!" even in the grounds. He curtly demanded payment and growled that photography was also "*Interdit!*"

The painted interior of the church was troubling, depicting people having stakes hammered up their bottoms or their backs ploughed by devils. It rather reflected the welcome. I ran back up the hill with 4 lei that I had collected from Mark and told the keyholder that "*Mon mari* – my husband" would not bother to look inside.

We drove back via Glod, evidently the filming location for Borat's home village, supposedly in Kazakhstan. The guidebooks designated Glod as a 'pretty village' even though its name means 'mud'. Unfortunately, viewing it through eyes clouded by the unashamed loveliness of Breb, we were a little disappointed. However, the state of the road was comparable. It was very steep and very unmade. We are reasonably confident that we didn't drive on any footpaths, but we couldn't be sure.

It had been a gorgeous day filled with sunshine, glorious artistry and the atmosphere of a pastoral paradise.

The following day, we planned to explore Breb properly. We could hardly wait.

43

BLOWN AWAY BY BREB – OUR LAST DAY IN ROMANIA

We Walk the Enchanted Way

It was the last day of September. There was a morning frost and rain in the forecast. A decision was made; it would be our last day in Romania. We loved Breb and would have happily stayed there, but we didn't want to get stranded.

Besides worries about the weather, a further dog-transport panic arose. Although Breb is but a whisper away from Ukraine, we couldn't cross the border with the pooches. A titer test is needed for Ukraine, which doesn't recognise a three-year rabies vaccination either. Serbia requires a titer test, we knew that but also caught a hint about it being necessary for Hungary when entering from a high-risk rabies country. Hastily, we checked alternative exit points, but it also applied to Bulgaria and Moldovia. We were trapped!

We consulted Evelyn.

"We had a guest whose passport ran out. She was refused at one border crossing but simply went to the next one and was waved through."

So, we could try different check-points until one let us through. Well, at least it was a plan. Further panicky research revealed that only the UK Government website listed Romania as a high-risk rabies country. Everyone had EU pet passports and the countries that we needed to cross were all EU. Technically, we should be fine...

It was either Blade's last day in his home country – or not.

For the rest of the beautiful, autumn day, we ambled around Breb. People were busy in the fields; they all waved to us and shouted their greetings, "*Buna!*" Some stopped us to chat away in Romanian, clearly bemused that people could exist on Earth who did not speak their language.

We passed the 'Prince Charles' houses, a street of traditional, wooden houses bought and preserved by the MET when Charles was its patron. They were charming, like gingerbread houses in a fairy tale, topped with shingle roofs, sitting in grounds of the most exquisite green and surrounded by woven, wooden fences.

Through lush gardens and orchards, we caught glimpses of fields full of hay ricks. Creasta Cocolusui smiled down on us; we vowed to return and hike there.

A fruity, alcoholic scent pervaded the air all around

the village. Every yard contained huge vessels, brimming with fermenting plums. The next batch of horincă in the making. Small signs on the walls of several houses advertised the craft speciality of the residents.

It was Sunday. Ladies walked back from church arm-in-arm, four or five abreast, grinning and chatting. In their traditional coloured skirts and headscarves, it was a sight that could not fail to make you smile. They all waved and greeted us warmly. We wandered down a shady lane by a stream to the wooden church of 'The St Archangels, Michael and Gabriel'. Breb is an old Romanian word for 'beaver' and harks back to times past when beavers dammed the mountain streams that flow through the village.

We were greeted by an elderly couple in traditional dress; the man had a tiny straw hat perched on top of his head, its decorative ribbons streamed down his back. Sadly, it was a sight that also foretold the relentless march of progress. The lady was holding a mobile phone.

Things are changing, even in Breb, where life has continued unaltered for centuries. Understandably, people are beguiled by the technology, ease and plenty of a more Western European lifestyle. But it encourages envy and, amid the drive for advancement and possession, it is too easy to lose sight of what is most precious, to underestimate the value of intangible things that money can never buy – and to fail to identify the point at which progress is no longer serving our best interests.

Like Evelyn and Matthias, we recognised Breb as a paradise. If we were looking to settle down, we could certainly see ourselves in Breb. Had we found it a few years ago, before we got the travel bug, perhaps we might already have been there, living in a tree house above a river with the pups and a Lipizzaner each.

We wanted it to stay the way it was. Not to allow tourists like us to gawp at the horses and carts or the quaint people tilling the fields by hand. Our fear was that a priceless quality of life would be obliterated by the implacable drive to modernise – and missed only when it was lost forever.

Breb is the rural idyll that the already-modernised crave and seek out, a place where people have an identity and a sense of belonging. As we battle with our existential angst and endeavour to find new and inventive ways to go a little bit greener, all we need to do is look. In Romania, you can already see a community that has been happy, sustainable and self-sufficient for centuries.

We felt exceptionally lucky to have experienced this wonderful country before its culture and traditions had been consumed. Romania's beauty is so much more than historic buildings, pristine landscapes and vast tracts of wilderness. It is her people: their open kindness, their sense of community and the way that they interact with the land, in tune with nature and the rhythms of the seasons.

44

BREB TO BUDAPEST – LA REVEDERE ROMÂNIA

A Bum Steer in Budapest

Customs officials never smile back.

A translucent, mantis-like lady, with bleached hair scraped back in a ponytail, cast a cursory look into Big Blue's cab.

"Three," she announced.

I decided not to enlighten her. I just flashed her the smile that was not returned.

Approaching the Hungarian border, we had sailed past several kilometres of HGVs, nose to tail. It was a single-track road, but we slipstreamed our way past the lorries in the wake of an unladen flat-bed. When in Romania...

Waiting in the queue at the border, our hearts were thumping. Would we fall foul of requirements for a titer test? Would Blade's Romanian passport be acceptable?

Ruby likes to travel tucked up in her little bed behind the seats and we were happy that she stayed there, out of sight. Blade lay on a black rug, which helped him to blend into the background. We had nothing to hide, but saw no need to solicit unnecessary attention.

Officials checked inside the caravan and the back of the van, marvelling at all our windsurfing equipment. A German couple in a car opposite waved furiously at us and the dogs. If we were really serious smugglers, we could have made ourselves a little less conspicuous.

We sailed through without having to produce any pet passports.

...

Imagine the culture shock of leaving a village in the Middle Ages, driving for eight hours, then entering a major city in rush hour with a defunct Naffsat and no detailed city map. As if the worry of getting dogs across the border were not enough, we had to tow a large caravan through a labyrinth of roads as it was going dark and try to locate an out-of-the-way campsite in the hills. After which, our only challenge would be to pitch in darkness, with no jockey wheel.

Thankfully, the Hungarian M3 motorway spewed us on to the road we wanted, albeit heading in the wrong direction. We managed to effect a U-turn and cross a grey and angry-looking Danube from pancake-flat Pest into bosomy Buda. We swung a hasty left, to somewhere beginning with D that seemed not to feature on Google maps. In the absence of a map, Mark had written down the areas of the city that we needed to pass through to reach the campsite; Újlak, Zöldmál and Szépilona. Like 'D', none were signposted.

Navigating by laptop, the challenge was to make out the route and the road names on the screen and then give Mark directions as we wove our cumbersome bulk through rush hour. The conversation went thus:

"We need to turn left on Pac... Pac... I can't pronounce it. I'll spell it. P-a-c-s-i-r-t-a-m-e-z-ő útca."

"That doesn't help much."

"Let's just call it Pac Man. Oh look. Pac-something. We're on it! That was lucky. Next, we need, Sz. Sz. Crikey. Look out for a road that begins with Sz... (Szépvölgyi útca.)"

And so it continued as we crawled in twilight along narrow roads, dazzled by lights, snaking uphill through residential streets above the Danube. The map gave no inkling of the suitability of the roads for towing. I just had to look for a logical route from A to Z, since Zuglieget was our final destination.

I had my nose virtually glued to the computer screen. If I set the screen to show both the campsite and our location simultaneously, the road names were too small to read, so it became a feat of memory.

Remarkably, we got to Zuglieget and found ourselves directly outside the entrance of Campsite

Niche. Had I had any trace of a sense of humour remaining, I would have said in a robot voice "You Have Reached your Destination".

Mark likes to live on the edge. He had declined to bring the perfectly-sized log that had served us so well as a jockey wheel in Breb on the basis that, "We'll find something."

"It is almost exactly level!" I shouted as we reversed into our pitch in the dark. We agreed to leave the caravan hitched and seek a suitable jockey wheel substitute in daylight.

Camping Niche is an old tram terminus. The café in the old ticket office served food and more importantly beer. We needed beer. The lady who checked us in was delighted to welcome five dogs. She provided us with a complementary welcome beer and we ordered a Hungarian beef stew, which came with a slice of white bread. Then we ordered more beer.

Unrelated to these beers, Mark tripped in the night. He landed on the corner of the plastic dog food box and cracked his ribs, which left him struggling to move, never mind raise heavy objects. This was a phenomenally welcome turn of events when, in order to unhitch, we would need to lift the front of the caravan and support it by some means as yet to be foraged.

I guess that this is what they call adventure. It was all getting a bit much.

...

Eat, Play, Love – A Letter from Blade

I struck with the speed of a cobra! I took a pork chop straight off The Dogmother's plate as she reached for the salt and pepper. How was that for speed?! She wasn't too pleased, although afterwards she laughed about me eating off Wedgewood when she'd seen me climb inside a bin the other day. "You can take the dog off the street" she said. Anyway, it all worked out in the end. Everybody got a piece of the pork that had my teeth marks in it. I think the Frou Frous were quite chuffed with my efforts.

We've also been in the campsite restaurant. Everyone was impressed with how good and quiet I was. They bought me a chain lead so that I can't chew through it; however, during dinner, I managed to chew the handle right off Lani's lead and got half way through Rosie's new one.

The bed continues to be a battle ground. On the streets, persistence rarely let me down. It has taken just over a month but they did crack. They let me up there – and then told me off! Humans, huh?! They told me that I could never go on the bed again because I had chewed a load of holes in their new blankets. And they had been boasting that the blankets only cost €4 each.

I jumped up again yesterday morning and was quiet as a mouse. They let me stay and gave me lots of love. I don't think The Dogmother minds hoovering all the hair off – it's called fur-niture for a reason. I get now that they don't like lacy blankets, especially the new ones, so I left the blankets alone.

I am learning, see!

45

CROSSING THE CONTINENT -
HUNGARY, SLOVENIA, ITALY

We Reach Our City Limits

I often urge ladies to develop and maintain caravan towing skills and this is why.

We were in Budapest, 1,100 miles from home and my beloved was in too much pain to drive in a straight line, never mind manoeuvre or reverse. It could have been worse; we could have been stuck in Romania, waiting for snow to close the roads.

Since we were back in civilisation (Budapest is the seventh largest city in Europe) we availed ourselves of some facilities, sightseeing and some satnav shopping. We bought a new satnav, although the guys in the shop fixed Naffsat, so that we had a spare.

"What was wrong with it?" I asked innocently.

"The connector had come loose. They soldered in a new one. It only cost £15 – half of what the manufacturer had quoted to look at it, never mind fix it."

So, the failure was not water-induced. I am a great believer in honesty between husband and wife. The time seemed right to admit to the dog bowl incident.

...

Budapest is a beautiful city and there were picturesque walks in the woodlands behind Campsite Niche. However, we finally reached our city limits when we spent a whole afternoon crawling around Pest in traffic, playing chicken with rattling, yellow trams, as we tried to buy some replacement leads and a new collar for Blade. Somehow, Blade had managed to lose his collar on our last day in Breb. I guess that he had just wanted to leave a memento of himself in his home country.

It was so much easier travelling with a satnav, although I got plenty of looks as I towed a long vehicle across three countries. Pulling out of Camping Niche, one man looked genuinely terrified when he saw a woman at the wheel. He rushed to hide behind his burger cart. I wonder what he would have thought if he knew that I could fly a plane.

Finally, we arrived at our old haunt, Camping Maroadi on Lake Garda, with a plan: fine Italian food, wine and sunshine for as long as it took for Mark's ribs to get better. And in the meantime, at least one of us could windsurf.

...

It was fortunate that I didn't know the Italian for "I want to marry you and have your babies." Otherwise I would have said it to the Site Maintenance Man. In passing, he had noticed our curious jockey wheel arrangement – not difficult, since it involved the caravan jack perched on a large tin of apricot halves – and volunteered to do something about it.

I made him a brew when he popped back with his tools. He drilled out the sheared bolt, welded the two halves back together and returned us to conventional jockey wheel action. He refused any money.

"*Caffè è basta*," he insisted. Coffee is enough.

With hindsight, perhaps it was just as well that I hadn't gone into the whole marriage and baby thing.

Although we had to avoid towing in the rain to keep our cracked and duct-taped caravan floor dry, our new satnav had conducted us safely back to the 21st century. We set off back to England, brimming with confidence.

So much so that we ate the apricot halves.

...

However, we were left with a dilemma. Where to go on our next trip – and how could it possibly surpass Romania?

EPILOGUE

A Letter to Blade

Dear Blade

We are so pleased that you are fitting in so well in England – even though you nearly didn't make it because the vet and the Customs lady both fell in love with you and wanted to keep you.

We miss you, but are so happy that you have found your forever home. It was wonderful to see how you bonded so spontaneously when you met our mates, Sally and Richard. It was clearly love at first sight – and strangely heart-warming to see that you went with them without a backward glance. When you know something's right, why hesitate? And we can still see you!

We love getting your updates and are very impressed that you have been boating. You are a proper sea dog. It is good to hear that you are chilled with their chickens and that you have been keeping Sally on her toes with her marathon training.

Lia told us that in December, it was -30°C in your home town near Sibiu. We are so happy that you came with us and that we were able to give you a better life.

The rest of the family is fine. Kismet's replacement axle is still good, even after Romanian roads, and her floor is fixed after the incident with a pothole. Big Blue is also OK. The oil that she sprayed over Kismet was down to a worn filter. Not an expensive fix.

Mark got his tattoo of the Dacian Wolf. It actually looks rather like you, which is a nice reminder – although you will be etched on our hearts forever.

We are all back to enjoying our lie-ins – you were certainly persistent in the Battle of the Bed. I have to admit that the Fab Four are relieved by the peace...

Romania should have been our last year touring. The plan had always been to travel for three years and then settle down. However, we still have itchy feet. We have to break the news that Mark has tours planned for at least the next twenty years.

We look forward to seeing you next time we are in Dorset.

Lots of love,

Jackie, Mark, Kai, Rosie, Ruby and Lani xx

ACKNOWLEDGMENTS

I would like to thank the following people;

Lia Howlett – for being our unfailing 'Voice of Reason' when our Romanian resolve was slipping.

Blade – you proved that not only Romania but also its dogs defy stereotypes.

Sally and Richard Marshall – for welcoming Blade into the most perfect active and loving home. You are Blade's happy ending.

Nicky Crowe – www.nickycrowe.com for doggie training tips for Blade.

Debbie Purse – at Book Covers for You for bringing 'Dogs 'n' Dracula to life in pictures.

Carol Dewhurst – whom I have known since the age of ten, for your valued friendship as well as ensuring that my grammar didn't let the grammar school girls down!

Caroline Smith – for eagle-eyed proofing and beta reading of my manuscript.

Sophie Wallace – @SophieWallaceProofreading for support and advice beyond the call of duty, as well as ever perfect and painstaking proofing.

Jennifer Barclay – for editing my Romanian ramblings.

Elizabeth Barlow-Hall – www.libbysworld.fiveotherwise.com for creating the wonderful map of our Romanian Road Trip.

To My Readers Around the World – as authors, we bare our souls for your entertainment. Your kind words, reviews and encouragement mean so much.

And of course, Mark, Kai, Rosie, Ruby and Lani for filling every day with love and joy.

And Finally – A Request

Even more than a duct-taped caravan floor, functioning jockey wheel and a benign satnav, as an author, I rely on your reviews.

I aim to entertain and inform – and hopefully inspire. If I got close, I would be unbelievably grateful if you could leave a review on Amazon.

No essays required. Even a single sentence would be greatly appreciated.

Dog Bless You All

ABOUT THE AUTHOR

The New Family Shot – Blade's first on-lead excursion to St Michael's Church, Cisnădioara. The Author with husband Mark and the Fab Four, Kai, Rosie, Ruby and Lani.

Jacqueline Lambert is a fanatical windsurfer, skier and northerner, who can ride a horse, fly a plane and tow a caravan. Her claims to fame are fire-eating on Japanese TV and sharing both a home town and once, a swing, with World Superbike champ, Carl Fogarty – 'The Blackburn Bullet' – who lived across the road when they were both nine.

A biochemist with adventure in her DNA, she rafted, rock-climbed and backpacked around six continents before giving up the day job to travel full-time with her husband and four dogs. Now, she is a dedicated doggie travel blogger and author of *Fur Babies in France* and *Dog on the Rhine*, a tome which totters occasionally into the 'No 1 Bestseller' list for German Travel.

@JacquelineLambertAuthor
www.WorldWideWalkies.com

Printed in Great Britain
by Amazon